*"Sitting in front of Mount Jingting*
*The birds fade away while flying upwards*
*A solitary cloud moves in a grand nonchalance*
*Alone, we remain face to face, Mount Jingting and I*
*Without ever growing tired of one another."*

Li Bai

# PRANLAS-DESCOURS

## DEPTH OF THE LANDSCAPE

jovis

# FOREWORD

Throughout the history of civilizations, the relationship between architecture and landscape has been the object of formulation, association, and sometimes opposition, depending on the ways in which societies have viewed themselves, and how they were projected and built. Even if we observe great fractures in the understanding of landscape through an architectural prism, we can nevertheless identify recurring figures that have been re-examined according to specific cultures and social organizations.

During the 16th and 17th centuries, mapped geography, which became more and more precise through the discovery of other continents, revealed that, rather than individual elements, there were entire landscapes where topography, hydrology, geology, and vegetation would no longer be considered as being isolated, but as globally related entities with precise descriptive codes.

For a long time, the conditions of each geographical situation, with agricultural soils and basic terrain conditions, informed the adaptation of architecture. And, at the same time, according to how societies were designed, architecture has maintained very different relationships between intellectual cultures and the representation of each civilization.

The philosophical principles kneaded together by Aristotle (or Heraclitus) formed the ancient model for considering architecture and landscape, where objects were disembodied from universal dimensions within the natural environment, subjecting architecture more to rational principles than to the injunctions of soil and climate. The order of the classical temple thus became an element for revealing landscape and imbuing it with meaning.

The radical dialogue between architecture and landscape is, of course, not limited to the ancient world, and has continued in many architectural cultures. In this respect, Mies van der Rohe is one of the contemporary heroes of the 20th century. However, one can perceive in ancient cultures an innate sense of adaptation: the amphitheaters are striking examples of this capacity, with cultural nuances like those mentioned by Laurence Durrell: "the Greek amphitheater is built for the ear and the sound, the Roman amphitheater for the eye and the image."[1]

From Palladian villas to the landscape projects of André Le Nôtre, harmonious regulations of our landscape have been developed through rational layouts and the preeminence of architectural orders (Lenfant's Washington DC foundation is a perfect archetype).

From the industrial period at the end of the 19th century and throughout the 20th, powerful contemporary planning tools obviated the need to negotiate the constraints of landscape or respect its alterities. The decomposition of contemporary landscapes across the planet by an accumulation of unrelated infrastructures has given rise to hybrid, involuntary, and enigmatic accumulations, revealing dismay in our society's view of itself. Nature finds itself damaged and bruised, and tragedies accumulate from year to year: floods, pollution, hurricanes, fires, and at times, the entire destruction of ecosystems.

The divorce between natural landscapes and "planning" undertaken with brutal technical forces has caused the loss of nature's most beneficial elements, the very qualities that are sought after. For so long now, we have witnessed a partition within our landscape between safeguarded and protected sectors (a form of museography where landscapes are separate and immobilized in canonical biodiversity) and the rest is largely abandoned to the mercy of technical development and unbridled capitalism.

Farmers have used the word "resilience" when calling for the creation of new conditions for the use of agricultural land, after each of these events that they have had to endure. Undoubtedly, an alliance must be born in order to reinvent technical tools to build contextualized landscape narratives and to help reverse climate change (A Tale of Water, Yuzhong).

In this book, projects for housing, public facilities, and urban territory projects are grouped together in order to illustrate an approach which, through different situations, raises the question of the relationship between preserved or post-industrial landscapes and architecture for classic uses. Through these diverse projects, the design of architectural space is questioned by the depth of landscape with the desire to engage and qualify these architectural spaces in an intense and honor-bound relationship with the natural habitat and post-industrial landscapes.

This theme is a common thread starting with the initial urban project for the creation of the city center of Saint-Jacques-de-la-Lande, (1992–2018) which, through the design of its urban layouts, seeks to embody the surrounding landscape of the Vilaine Valley. In Lille, opposite the Botanical Garden, this narrative continues until the most recent project of the Chamber of Trades and Crafts for the Hauts-de-France (Chambre des Metiers).

Examining the depth of landscape has shown to be an optimistic approach to the contemporary conditions of each site, even the most degraded ones, in an attempt to reinvent and resuscitate all things elementary and primitive in the creation of architecture, and the joy that it therefore brings.

[1] Durrell, Lawrence: Sicilian Carousel. London 1977.

Chambre de Métiers et de l'Artisanat, Lille, France

# TRANSFORMATION IN THE EXPANDED FIELD

Ashley Simone

"Architecture does not begin with the primitive hut but with the marking of ground."

Vittorio Gregotti (1983)

On an October day in 2021, I found myself in Lille, France, standing in a wooded garden with the architect Jean-Pierre Pranlas-Descours. This garden, a modest version of the nearby Jardin des Plantes, is situated east of the Chambre de Métiers et de l'Artisanat (Chamber of Trades and Crafts) or CMA, which is a mixed-use building, completed in 2019, built to the designs of Pranlas-Descours in collaboration with the Dutch practice KAAN Architecten and structural engineer David Chambolle, with whom Pranlas-Descours has worked for more than 20 years. A winding dirt path made inconspicuous by its indefinite boundary links the garden with CMA, a somewhat anonymous, three-story Neo-Miesian building. The concrete and steel structure of the building is clad in stone and glass and organized over three floors, the middle story being inset between the ground and second floors. This first-floor setback provides for a partially covered terrace, five meters in width on all sides but for the north façade, where the roof of the building at ground level is generously and obliquely extended past the square cantilevered upper floor so that the terrace—visible from the garden—aligns to the trace of a former railway line. The ground plane of this outdoor space is paved in concrete slabs of four different sizes, yielding a pattern that is characteristic of an obsessive approach to the precise modulation of the materials used throughout the building.

An equally modular precision is evident in the double-glazed windows which make up the continuous perimeter envelope of the CMA, where they are separated from each other by thin, polished aluminum mullions. A reflective screen print, with a gradient that dissipates at eye level, is applied to the fenestration throughout,

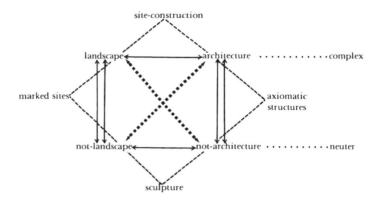

Rosalind Krauss, Diagram, Sculpture in the Expanded Field

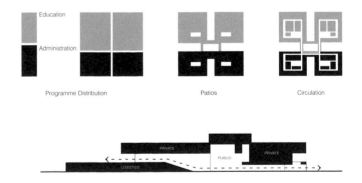

Diagram, the Organization of Programs,
CMA in Lille, France (2019)

which has the effect of creating a surface that operates as a mirror reflecting the surrounding context in the building's envelope. From the vantage of the garden, the earth feels soft underfoot and nature fuses with architecture on the surface of the structure where white-bark birch trees are fractured in their transposition from the landscape to the building's exterior. Seen from the park, the building seems to oscillate between landscape and architecture, quite literally exemplifying what Rosalind Krauss identified as the expanded field of sculpture, as seen in the work of Donald Judd.[1]

Perceived in its totality, however, the building's manifest preoccupations with social and environmental concerns defies it being reduced to the formal complexity identified by Krauss. The transposition of nature, which takes place on the glazed exterior of the structure, is palpably amplified within through courtyard plantings, the application of wood and stone revetment, and the amplification of natural light. This reception and presence of nature, inside and out, establish a resonant context that echoes the social and cultural transformations which the building has been designed to facilitate. A commitment to the public realm is characteristic of Pranlas-Descours' production throughout his career. In this regard, the CMA building in Lille is typical of his work that is equally preoccupied with the sensitive and artful marking of ground and engagement of both the formal and the historical context, irrespective of whether it be urban, suburban, or natural.

Remnants of a former 17th-century Vauban fortification lie under Rue Abélard, the high-speed ring road from which the CMA is approached. This topographic context recalls Pranlas-Descours' book *Density, Architecture and Territory* (2016) in which historical images of fortified cities from the 13th and 14th centuries, i.e. *The Expulsion of Demons from Arezzo* by Giotto and *The Allegory of Good and Bad Government* by Ambrogio Lorenzetti, are interspersed with contemporary images conveying present-day megalopolitan conditions. The implication of comingling past and present is that cities, built across centuries, are complex amalgamations of culture, politics, and spatial form that share a particular performative quality; they provide protection for human well-being in tangible and intangible ways. Space must be planned, government monumentalized, and individuals and communities cultivated. The forms and means of protection, of course, have evolved over time in accordance with shifting needs. The presence and visual absence of the Vauban fortification close to the CMA building is but one manifestation of the way in which civic tradition may be subtly sustained across time. Historically, cities have provided spaces of public appearance, where ideas can be exchanged, and the community rendered visible. In its totality, the CMA may be seen as a contemporary, compensating microcosm for the overall absence of the urban condition in Lille.

Two semi-public squares accessible to building users provide access to programming which can be approached directly from Rue Abélard located at the south of the site. Students entering the educational facilities (hairdressing, cooking, hospitality, and technology) do so by way of a ramp that connects to the first-floor terrace from the southwest corner of the site. Theater and concertgoers may gather on this same terrace before and after performances using doors at the back of the auditorium that open to the north. Office workers dedicated to local and regional arts administration enter the building on the central north-south axis of the 80 × 80 meter footprint, between two shallow pools, set parallel to a row of trees. A visual connection between the two semi-public entry spaces can be made due to the layering of spatial volumes, passing from the southern entrance hall to the auditorium, and to the northern section of the terrace. This spatial transparency is modulated in relation to the various conditions required by the programming. The sightline across the building's central north-south axis is mediated by an internal, retractable sunshade covering the southern glass wall of the auditorium, separating the stage from the entry hall. Here, a certain resonance between exterior and interior becomes evident, varying so that which may at first appear as monolithic may in fact disappear as one passes through space. While the building's glass envelope shifts according to its opacity, initially appropriating the landscape as surface and dissolving into literal transparency depending on contingent lighting conditions, transparency is at play in a phenomenal sense within the interior.[2] Volumes appear and disappear according to varying lighting conditions as one passes through the building, while the behavior of light generates the notion that the seemingly monolithic volume may be porous.

The porosity of the building is revealed by the plans and sections which show nine symmetrical openings cut through all three levels of the concrete structure. These perforations introduce natural light into the interior by way of three skylights and six internal courtyards. The natural light that enters the building via skylights is diffused by a suspended ceiling of opalescent glass at the double-height entry hall and in the auditorium by operable panels which are present above housings for the lights. The latter afford that the auditorium may be lit entirely by natural light or alternatively transformed into a black-box condition.

The largest courtyards are inserted between the auditorium and southern façade, where they are visible, respectively, through a fully glazed wall that opens onto the entrance hall.  Paving in Vals Quartzite extends through these glazed walls, into the adjacent courtyards, and onto the enclosing walls, which are punctured by long narrow windows held in place by thick, polished aluminum mullions. The sense of space is at its most monumental in the entry hall, where the suspended ceiling of opalescent glass, symmetrically located, appears as the contemporary equivalent of a Palladian dome. This effect is further emphasized by the large courtyards that project out left and right, perpendicular to the hall's central north-south axis. Here, the monumentality emphasized by the quartzite pavement, which assumes a gray or green hue derived from the color of the sky, is amplified by the articulation of stone around fenestration openings that rise from the bottom of each floor slab.

The openings at the first and second floors are two-thirds the height of those on the ground floor but share the same width. Above the ground and first floors,

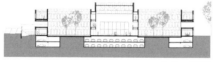

Section of CMA

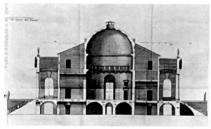

Section Drawing of Villa Rotonda by Andrea Palladio

Ashley Simone

groups of three narrow stone modules, half the height of the windows below which they appear, share a width dimension with the adjacent aluminum mullions and alternate horizontally with groups comprising three wider modules.

The level of detail demonstrated at the courtyards adjacent to the entry hall is also present at the other four courtyards, which are smaller in scale and distributed equidistantly to the north and south of the interior volume, and across the east and the west axis of the building. Each instance is analytically conceived and meticulously composed while being characteristic of an objective approach to formal, structural, and material articulation that is present across the entire structure and in its volumetric organization. Wood, including oak, birch, and bamboo, plus stone are variously used to line floors and walls along with the stone paving. The material layering that first appears in the double-glazing of the façade—lined on the inside with a third layer consisting of roller blinds—is further echoed in the interior by way of thin-membered steel railings, powder-coated white.

The volumetric layering that is evident in the double-height, open-plan entrance hall at the first floor gives way to more densely aggregated volumes of office space and educational programming. Procession through the building reveals even more layers such as the horizontal layering on the first floor where concealed steel trusses supporting the concrete slab at the second floor participate in generating a spatial compression that may be felt in a visceral and corporeal sense as one moves out from under the cantilevered second floor, across the northern terrace, and toward the garden.

The overall character of the façade and the dignity bestowed upon the users via the phenomenological effects of the building bring the work of Mies van der Rohe to mind. In many respects, it may be read as a collage of techniques and effects characteristic of Mies at different moments in his career, such as the reflection and dematerialization of glass. This appears in his building projected for Friedrichstrasse, Berlin in 1921, where the façade oscillates between translucency and transparency. Surely, the most salient comparison to Mies is to be found in the resonance between the CMA building and Mies' projection for the Illinois Institute of Technology in Chicago (1939). In this scheme, Mies attempted to generate a micro-urban condition with individual volumes that exhibit symmetry and, in certain instances, involve the physical occupation of architecture by nature plus the mirroring effects of glass that suggest ephemeral presence.

Pranlas-Descours has also played an extensive role as a planner in Lille as is evident from his attempt to revitalize the pre-and post-industrial landscape. On that October day in Lille, after leaving the CMA with the architect, we made our way along the Canal de la Deûle to a work-live district west of the city center. Here, greenery is cultivated by digging shallow canals along the perimeter of residential fabric to collect rainwater into tanks. The detail is a familiar one, seen in housing districts the architect has planned across France, where he similarly is seeking to respond to

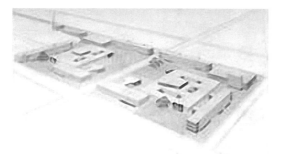

Mies van der Rohe, Scheme for the Illinois Institute of Technology in Chicago (1939)

Mies van der Rohe, Early Study for the Library and Administration Building, Illinois Institute of Technology, Chicago, Illinois, Perspective (c.1941–1944)

and transform the current urban condition and the lives of those who occupy it. In each instance, the environmentally conscious design attempted by a penumbra of vegetation tends to soften the boundary between public and private space.

Inserted into the brick-faced fabric of Lille's industrial era are two office buildings designed by Pranlas-Descours. Both buildings, the Bretagne and the Black Diamond, intervene and mark the Rives de la Haute-Deûle district with form and material, including metal, glass, and concrete that are foreign to the vernacular. While the materials and forms differ from the masonry constructs typical of the region's 19th-century fabric, which has undergone total transformation over the past 15 years, Pranlas-Descours has designed the office buildings such that they respectfully acknowledge and memorialize the past while introducing totally new forms of expression.

The Bretagne demonstrates contextual awareness in terms of both massing and detailing. The building's massing steps down across two floors, creating a wood-lined terrace with planks set on the oblique at the southeast where the building sits adjacent to a row of brick houses. In a converse gesture, the upper three floors northeast project out toward the former Leblan-Lafont factory, a castle-like fortress made of red brick. In terms of detailing, the vertical pleating of the façade's pre-cast concrete panels facilitates, through horizontal offset, a banding that generates the possibility for visually negotiating the transition between the surrounding context that comprises low-rise housing and the Leblan-Lafont factory, which has been repurposed with its interior hollowed out and retrofitted for retail programming.

Model of the Bretagne Office Building

At the Black Diamond office building, a sawtooth form of glass and black lacquered metal rises from a partially sub-grade red-brick base that accommodates parking for the mixed-use building above, containing offices and a sports facility. The detailing of the red-brick parking garage includes brise-soleil which blocks light and provides ventilation for the parking while celebrating, through its materiality, the industrial and cultural past of the Rives de la Haute-Deûle district.

Outside the city center of Nantes, which is located to the southwest of Lille, Pranlas-Descours collaborates with the city and governing bodies. The goal of the master civic plan is to affect the transformation of context and community by connecting the Cité de la Bottiére, a 50-year-old social housing district, with a programmatically diverse new district that includes housing, amenities, and infrastructure for sustainable practices including community gardens. The new district, for which Pranlas-Descours has designed housing, must also negotiate the existing residential fabric and a water body that bounds the site and supports wildlife, including birds, that enliven the built environment.

A médiatheque serves as a hinge between the old and new districts that are separated by rail lines. This new district and the replanning of Cité de la Bottiére are meant to offset urban sprawl, encourage exchange through programming public

Housing District, Bottière-Chenaie, Nantes

Ashley Simone

space, and draw young professionals and families to the region. As part of his civic collaborations, the architect designed 84 housing units that are distributed across two complexes located in the new district, and rendered in exposed and painted concrete. The first building comprises two- and three-bedroom units situated over six floors and assumes a sculptural character that carefully engages the ground with raw concrete panels that taper at the building's base. Responding to the topography, the building takes form in an irregular "U." The void created by the building's footprint originally framed an existing large-scale tree as it bent away from the street to create an internal courtyard and an elevated wooden plaza. The second building is a rectilinear form consisting of duplexes that are accessible via an internal courtyard and augmented with private gardens. Both buildings are conceived in a manner respectful of the existing streetscapes and natural topography. Situated amid ground marked with infrastructure for the collection of water and open ground belonging to wildlife or designated for public space, the desire that the buildings participate in environmental and social transformation is notably present. In this regard, the urban project, being developed over time, recalls Alvaro Siza's plan for Quinta da Malagueira in Évora, Portugal (1973–1977). Siza's vision sought to address issues of density while avoiding a *tabula rasa* approach and developing infrastructure and form in relation to the landscape with an ambition to instigate change through architecture.

Beyond the artful, sculptural approach to architecture that Pranlas-Descours demonstrates in skillfully marking ground with varied architectonic expressions, there is always a socially conscious dimension to his work. The intention to cultivate communities is palpable, as is a commitment to more sustainable forms of environmental interaction between built and natural landscapes. His work consistently attempts to go beyond the transformation of landscape to achieve a certain transformation of society.

Quinta da Malagueira, Evora, Portugal

[1] Krauss, Rosalind: "Sculpture in the Expanded Field." October, vol. 8, 1979, pp. 31–44.

[2] Rowe, Colin and Robert Slutzky: "Transparency: Literal and Phenomenal." Perspecta 8, 1963: 45.

# ARCHITECTURE

# TOPOGRAPHY

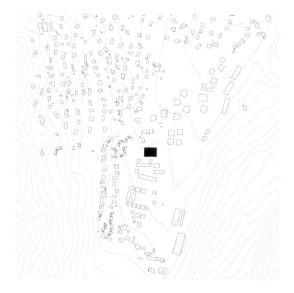

The construction of nine housing units in Seyssins (Grenoble) is part of the urban project of Pré Nouvel, a hilly landscape bordered by the Comboire forest found alongside a mountain river called "Les Galettes". The urban project consists of building 450 housing units over one decade around a new park. This new landscape is connected to the Alps mountain range with exceptional views of Mont Blanc.

Taking this into consideration, each different view looking out from the project was to be of the utmost importance. The creation of the different housing types is related to the particular topography and orientation of each situation.

On the edge of the park created around the river, the nine houses are developed on an artificial hill. This building is precisely adapted to the topography, as is the interior typological organization: two sets of four-bedroom dwellings on one level and five-bedroom duplex dwellings are inserted into the slope with enclosed private parking for all residents.

Access to the building is possible from the street in the west as well as directly from the park in the east. A communal garden is created west of the site compared to private gardens on the east side. The units are therefore developed from east to west around a central patio looking out onto three directions. The glass façades are entirely open, giving out onto vast terraces to the east and to the west. The exceptional qualities of the housing plan offer natural light throughout the day.

The structure combines three materials: glass on the east and west façades, stone on the north and south façades, and "corian" for the roofing and cladding. The combination of rough materials, such as stone, and smooth materials, such as glass or "corian" bring tension building with regards to its position within the site. A parking lot is integrated in the structure of the building with a private connection for several housing units.

The tectonic inscription of this building attempts to resonate with the large mountain landscape that circumscribes this exceptional site.

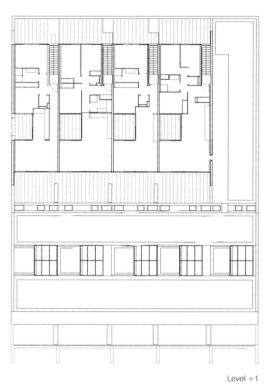

Level +1

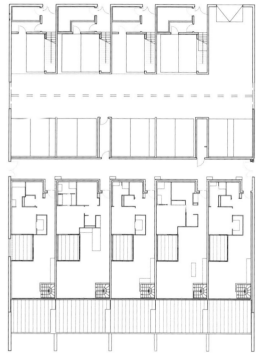

Entry Level

Level -1

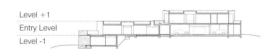

Level +1
Entry Level
Level -1

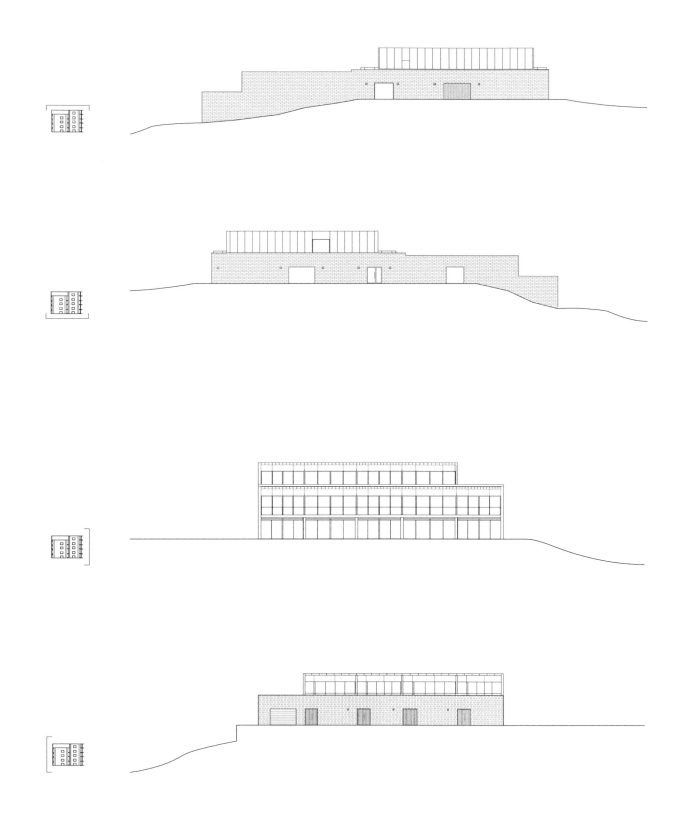

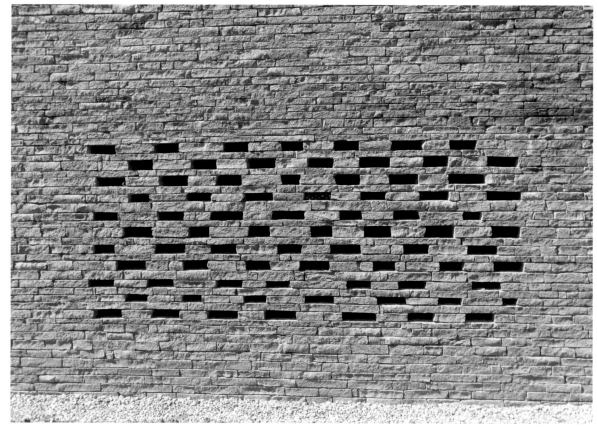

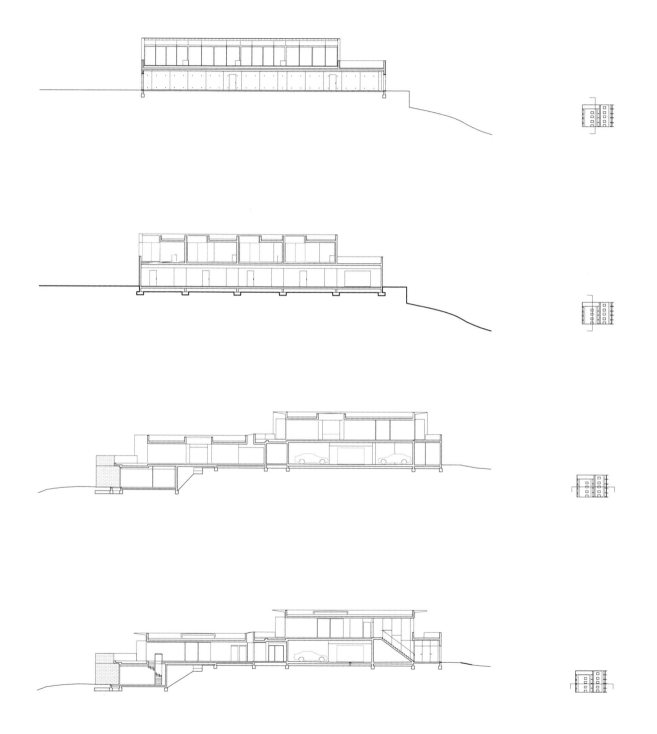

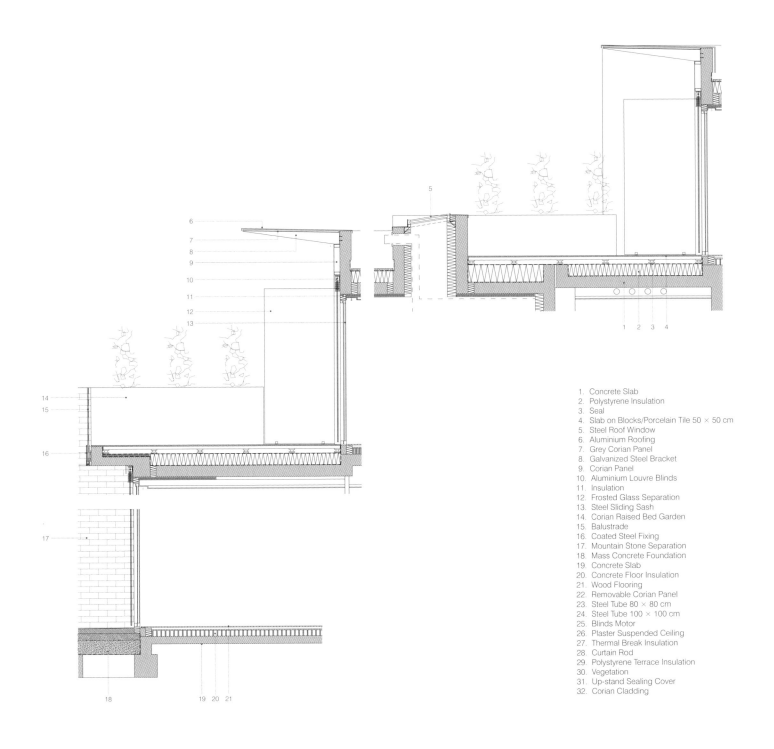

1. Concrete Slab
2. Polystyrene Insulation
3. Seal
4. Slab on Blocks/Porcelain Tile 50 × 50 cm
5. Steel Roof Window
6. Aluminium Roofing
7. Grey Corian Panel
8. Galvanized Steel Bracket
9. Corian Panel
10. Aluminium Louvre Blinds
11. Insulation
12. Frosted Glass Separation
13. Steel Sliding Sash
14. Corian Raised Bed Garden
15. Balustrade
16. Coated Steel Fixing
17. Mountain Stone Separation
18. Mass Concrete Foundation
19. Concrete Slab
20. Concrete Floor Insulation
21. Wood Flooring
22. Removable Corian Panel
23. Steel Tube 80 × 80 cm
24. Steel Tube 100 × 100 cm
25. Blinds Motor
26. Plaster Suspended Ceiling
27. Thermal Break Insulation
28. Curtain Rod
29. Polystyrene Terrace Insulation
30. Vegetation
31. Up-stand Sealing Cover
32. Corian Cladding

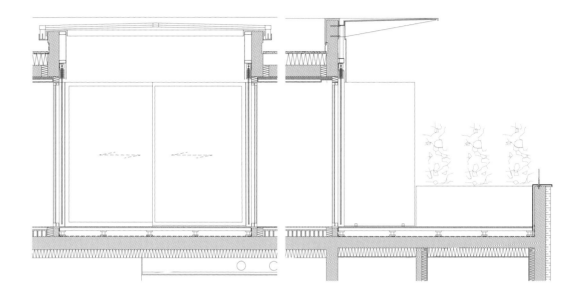

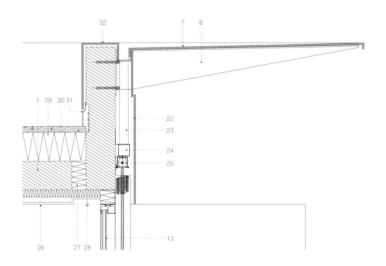

# PRIMITIVE LANDSCAPE

*"This building, the Guiding Swan, is dedicated to the Huldufólk, the hidden people who live within the rocks, walls, caverns, crevices, the Grjótagjá fissure, and swim in these warm waters with the ancient ones, the elegant swans, Iceland's beautiful maidens, who over the years determined the deaths of those in battle."*

The juxtaposition of tectonic plates and the three volcanic points surrounding the Grjótagjá cave offer an initiatory experience to the Icelandic landscape. The continental rift harkens back to the primitive formation of the earth's crust, to the telluric and hidden powers within the soil itself, an elemental figure upon which we walk. The relationship between these different sites, from the centre of the earth with its hot springs, to the tops of the volcanoes, justifies the implementation of an architectural structure that allows us to gradually discover this vast landscape.

Reinforcing tourist attraction in a place such as this seems obvious. For this reason, we have proposed a scenario throughout the project that directly confronts the scale of the site in four successive sequences:

1. The first sequence marks a direct contact with the contrast in height between the American plate and the European plate. This sequence takes place or is experienced within the building where the stone and the height difference from the fissure is framed.
2. The second sequence is developed from the terrace. From there, one can admire the extensive landscape of the Grjótagjá fissure, alongside the northwestern Krafla volcano on the horizon.
3. The third sequence, discovered when climbing up the tower, opens towards the southwest and the Hverfjall volcano.
4. The fourth and final sequence occurs once the visitor has reached the top of the tower and opens up the entire panoramic landscape with a new discovery of the Krafla volcano and Lake Myatn.

At the top of the tower a beam of light emerges, identifying the structure as a maritime lighthouse during the darker periods of the year. The construction, as a whole, aims to address and respect the landscape whilst becoming an architectural landmark within the vastness of the pre-existing site.

3

4

## Insertion Programs

The structure is implemented parallel to the Grjótagjá fissure, with all but the emerging tower aligned by height, thus highlighting the linearity of the site. This parallel volume is positioned at an equal distance from two entrances, leading into the fissure.

From the car park, itself reorganized as part of the project, a covered path along the architectural structure leads to a reception terrace to the northeast where several directions can be taken. These different paths around and throughout the building carefully and gently diffuse the tourists and bathers to prevent overcrowding on the site, as well as offering different experiences depending on the time they wish to dedicate to their discovery. As to the reorganization of the outdoor car park, the proposal aims to slightly bury this zone — by approximately one meter — so as to conceal the cars and other vehicles from view as visitors arrive.

The tower gives way to a particular experience, gradually revealing the landscape. The tower's envelope contributes to this revelation with wooden cladding allowing various transparencies and opacities depending on the façades.

## Construction and Sustainability

The construction of this structure makes use of two principal materials: stone and wood. In order to inscribe this building within the landscape, a platform for the car park is excavated so as to conceal the cars within the global landscape. The excavated stone will be recuperated to form gabion walls, constituting the opaque walls of the ground floor. Geothermal energy will provide the energy for heating and electricity for this building with electric charging stations installed in the car park.

Locally sourced wood constitutes the rest of the structure of the whole building, with certain metal connecting pieces used in order to assemble the wooden elements. The whole structure would be pre-prepared in a factory, as if it were a large Meccano kit, to be later assembled on site, thus minimizing intervention time on the site, in relation to the climatic conditions, and to reduce any impact on the landscape. Pre-assembled burnt wood cladding would form the external envelope of the structure.

Stone slabs, echoing the stone of the landscape, would cover the reception terrace and the interior. The exterior wooden deck walkways will be discreetly lit.

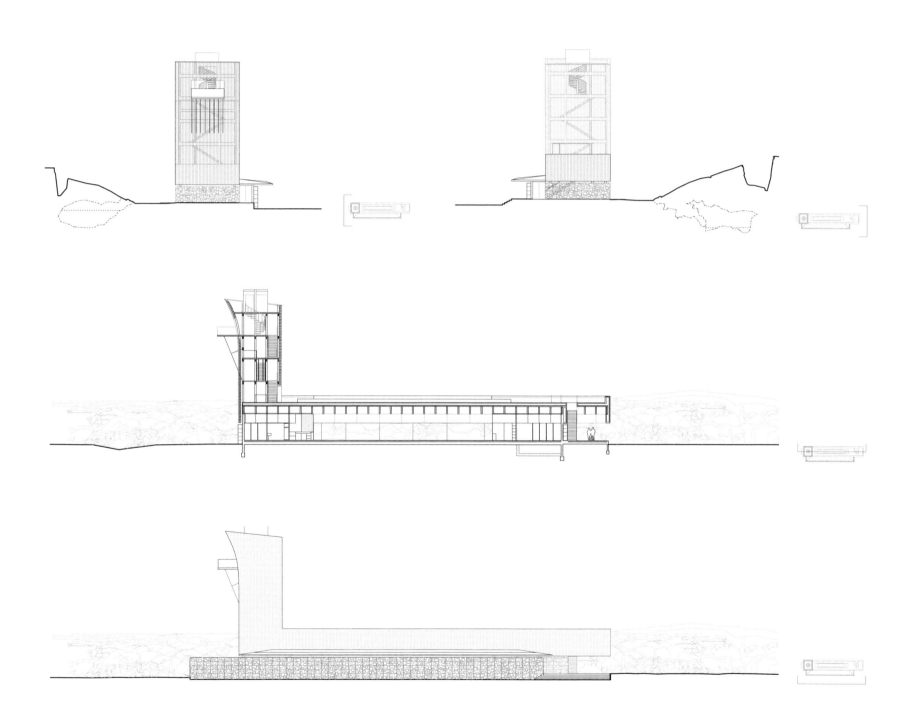

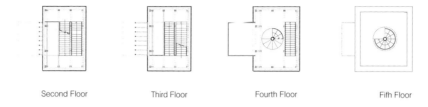

Second Floor          Third Floor          Fourth Floor          Fifh Floor

First Floor

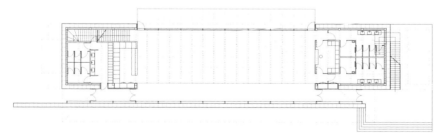

Ground Floor

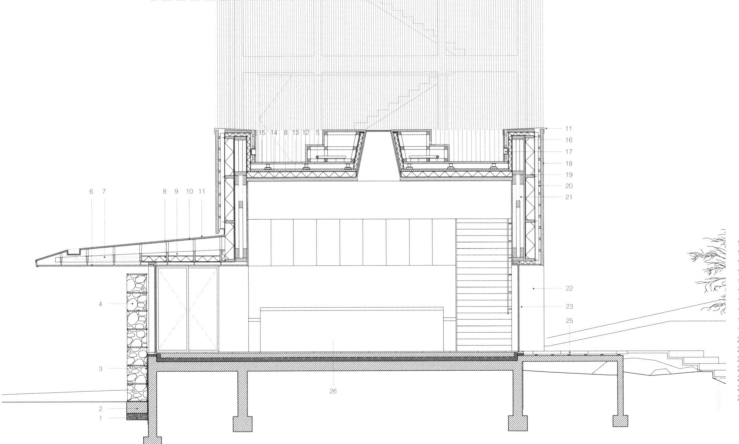

1. Fine Aggregate Bed (Gravel)
2. Reinforced Concrete Footing
3. Water Proofing Membrane
4. Gabion
5. Steel Beam: UPN 200
6. Ceiling Made of Wooden Cladding
7. Gutter Made of Smooth Metal Sheet
8. Insulation: Glass Wool 150
9. Wooden Beam
10. Sheet of Wood
11. Finishing: Metal Sheet Gutter
12. Adjustable Plot 150
13. Concrete Slabs 50
14. Cross-laminated Timber 110
15. Wood Decking
16. Outdoor Recessed Light
17. Wood Boarding
18. Burnt Wood: Yakisugi
19. Insulation:Glass Wood 250
20. Wooden Slats
21. Wooden Main Beam
22. Gabion Cladding Made of Wood
23. Climate Double Glazing
24. Concrete Slabs 100
25. Polished Stone Slab 80
26. Floor:
    - Polished Stone Slab 30
    - Concrete Slab Floor 120
    - Floor Heating System
    - Extruded Polystyrene 100
    - Concrete Slab 250

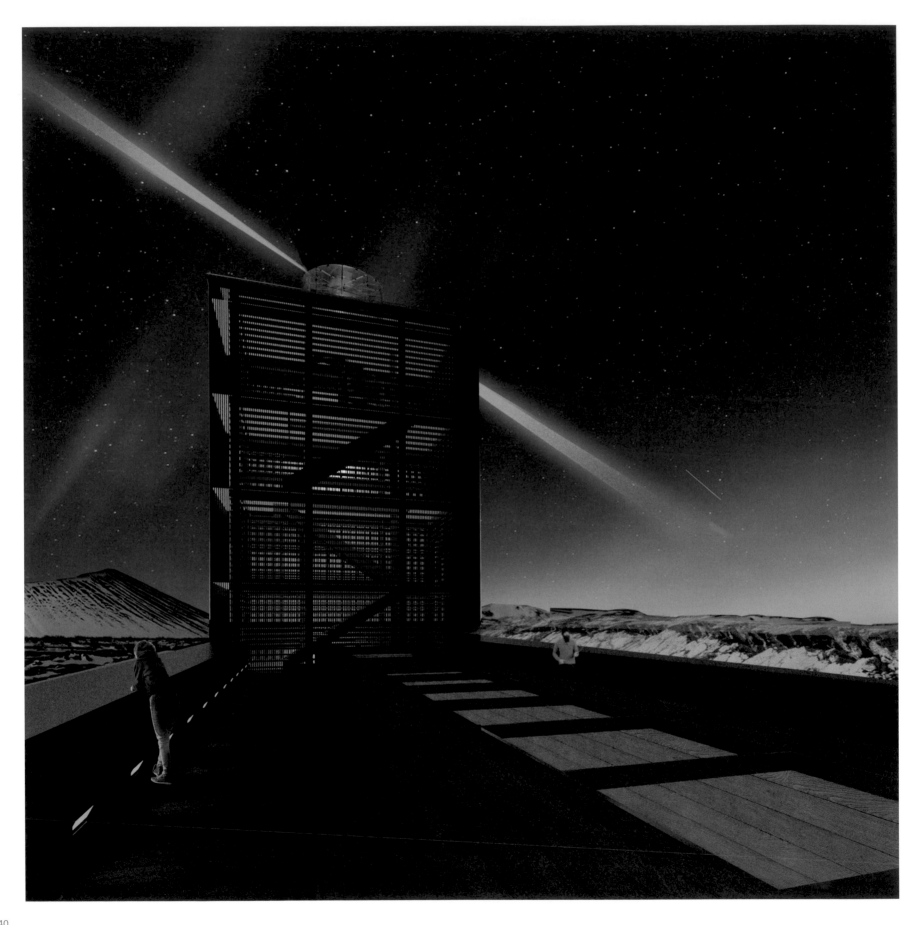

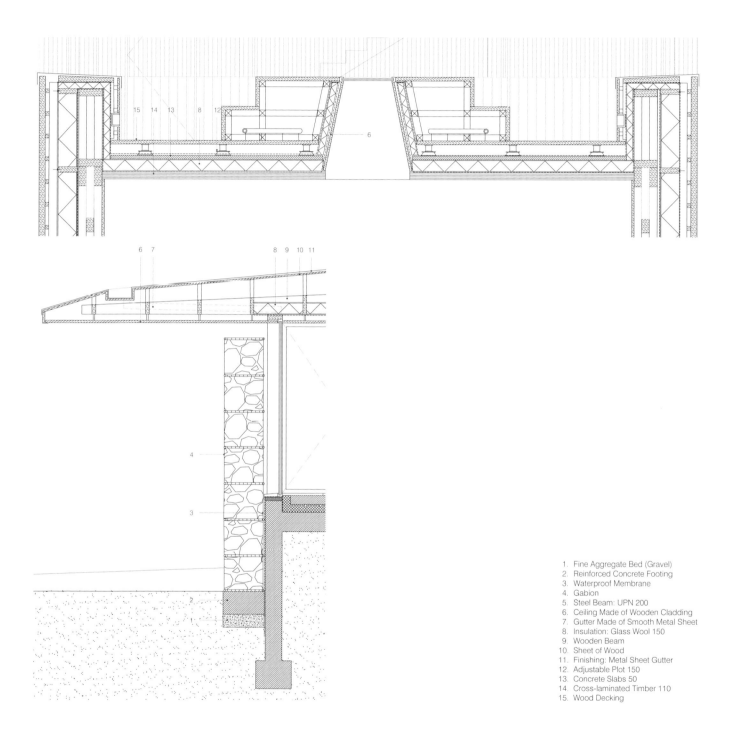

1. Fine Aggregate Bed (Gravel)
2. Reinforced Concrete Footing
3. Waterproof Membrane
4. Gabion
5. Steel Beam: UPN 200
6. Ceiling Made of Wooden Cladding
7. Gutter Made of Smooth Metal Sheet
8. Insulation: Glass Wool 150
9. Wooden Beam
10. Sheet of Wood
11. Finishing: Metal Sheet Gutter
12. Adjustable Plot 150
13. Concrete Slabs 50
14. Cross-laminated Timber 110
15. Wood Decking

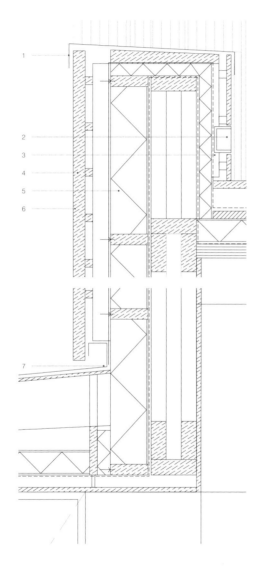

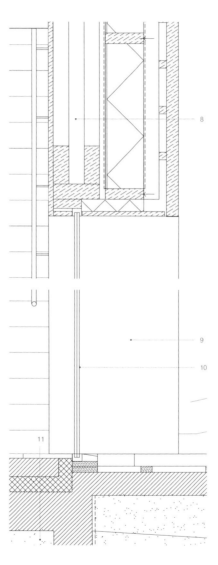

1. Finishing: Metal Sheet Gutter
2. Outdoor Recessed Light
3. Wood Boarding
4. Burnt Wood: Yakisugi
5. Insulation: Glass wood 250
6. Wooden Slats
7. Steel Beam: UPN 200
8. Wooden Main Beam
9. Gabion Cladding Made of Wood
10. Climate Double Glazing
11. Floor:
   - Polished Stone Slab 30
   - Concrete Slab Floor 120
   - Floor Heating System
   - Extruded Polystyrene 100
   - Concrete Slab 250

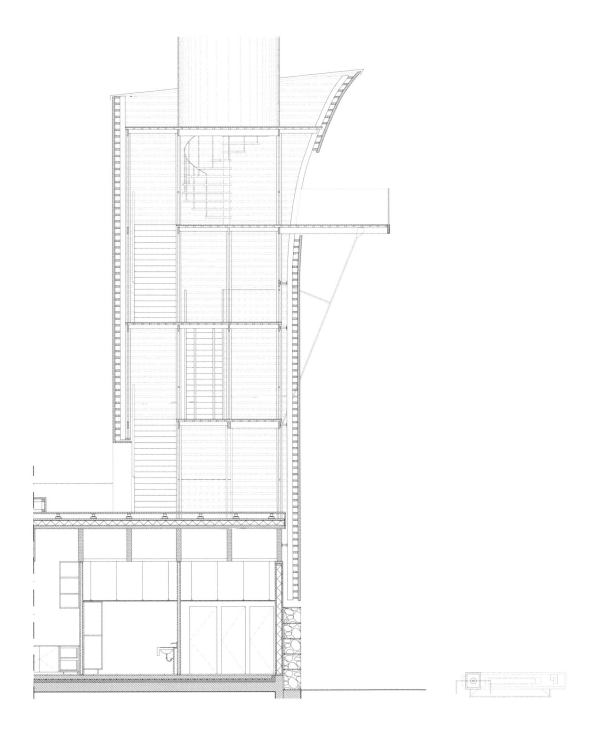

43

# INSIDE – OUTSIDE

The 32 housing units in Clamart are part of the renovation of the Cité du Pavé Blanc, an area primarily with social housing on the edge of the Meudon Forest in Western Paris. This project consists of rehabilitating pre-existing buildings on site (800 apartments) and redesigning public space as well as the construction of 84 new housing units. The 32-unit building develops a building type of grouped around a central courtyard, with two-bedroom units on the ground floor, and duplexes on the first and second floors.

Each unit extends onto a terrace, as well as an individual exterior patio for the duplexes. From the common central courtyard, each unit has an individualized entry, offering a strong sense of privacy for each resident within this ensemble of collective housing. Facing the surrounding landscape to the west and to the east, the apartments offer generous views, in particular, towards the peaceful and famous Robert Auzelle cemetery. Each room is bathed in natural light, including bathrooms and hallways.

The building is built using prefabricated white concrete walls for the exterior façades, and coated concrete for the inner courtyard. All windows are adorned with Venetian blinds with adjustable slats ensuring summer comfort, and limited views looking into the main rooms.

First Floor

Third Floor

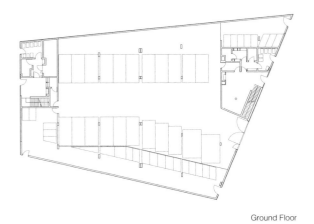

Ground Floor

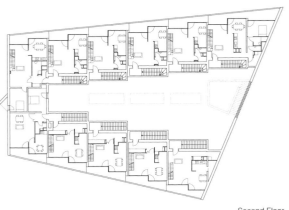

Second Floor

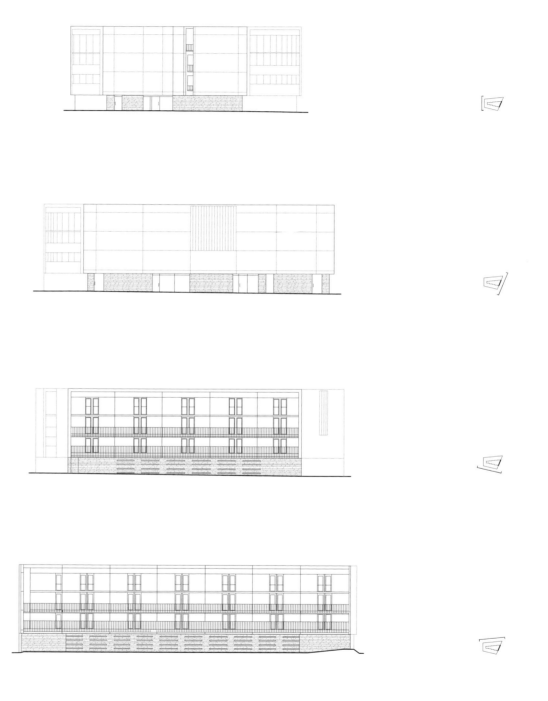

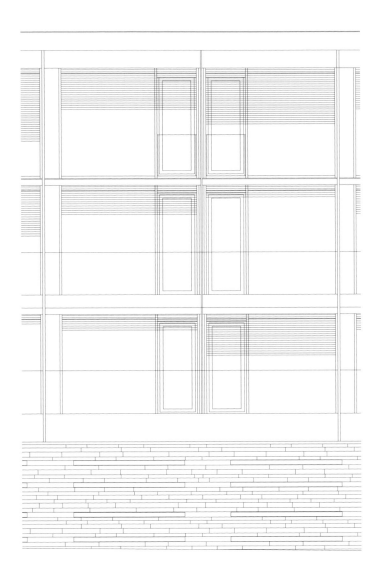

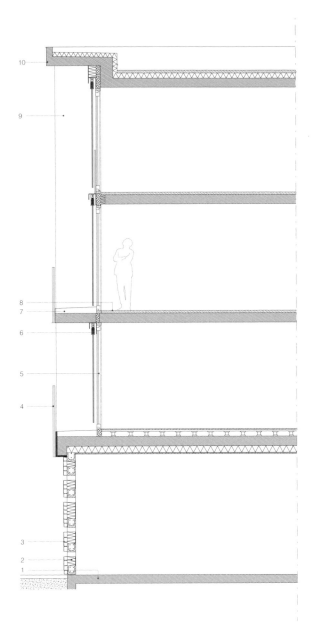

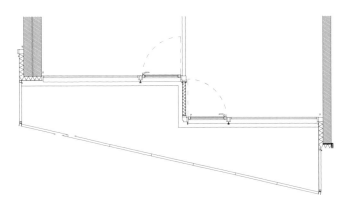

1. Concrete Slab
2. Structure: Concrete Block
3. Stone
4. Coated Metal Balustrade
5. Coated Aluminium Window Sash
6. Louvre Blinds
7. Concrete Floor Scrood
8. Soft Floor Finish
9. Coated Steel Separation
10. White Precast Element

1. Loggia
2. Bedroom
3. View of Patio From Inside
4. Patio

# NATURE AND ABSTRACTION

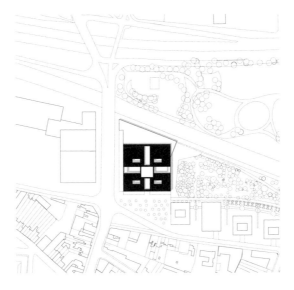

The Chamber of Trades and Crafts is set along the edge of the former 17th century Vauban fortification, now replaced by a high-speed ring road. The northern border of the site is defined by a railway line and the botanical garden — Jardin des Plantes de Lille. To the south, Rue Abélard defines the perimeter of a wider master plan area designed by KAAN Architecten and PRANLAS-DESCOURS architect comprising of Eurartisanat headquarters, five future buildings and a lush park spanning the site as an extension of the nearby garden.

With its minimalist esthetics and elegant transparency, the monolithic building provides an embracing and protective gesture towards the surrounding nature reinforcing the dialogue between the diverse elements of the area. In wide horizontal strokes, the Chamber of Trades and Crafts spreads over three floors rising from a square-shaped footprint of 80 by 80 meters and hosts both educational and administrative functions. Each floor holds a strong connection to the green landscape: on the first floor KAAN Architecten and PRANLAS-DESCOURS architect designed a prominent cantilever that frames a scenic view of Lille and the gardens.

The building features two public squares on different levels. On the ground floor is the new Place des Artisans (south), while a large terrace to the north of the first floor aligns the project with Rue du Faubourg d'Arras and connects to it by a bridge. Both public entrances are linked by an enfilade of representative spaces: southern square, entrance hall, the auditorium and its foyer, as well as a wide opening overlooking the north terrace. Moreover, each entrance serves the two main architectural realms: educational and administrative.

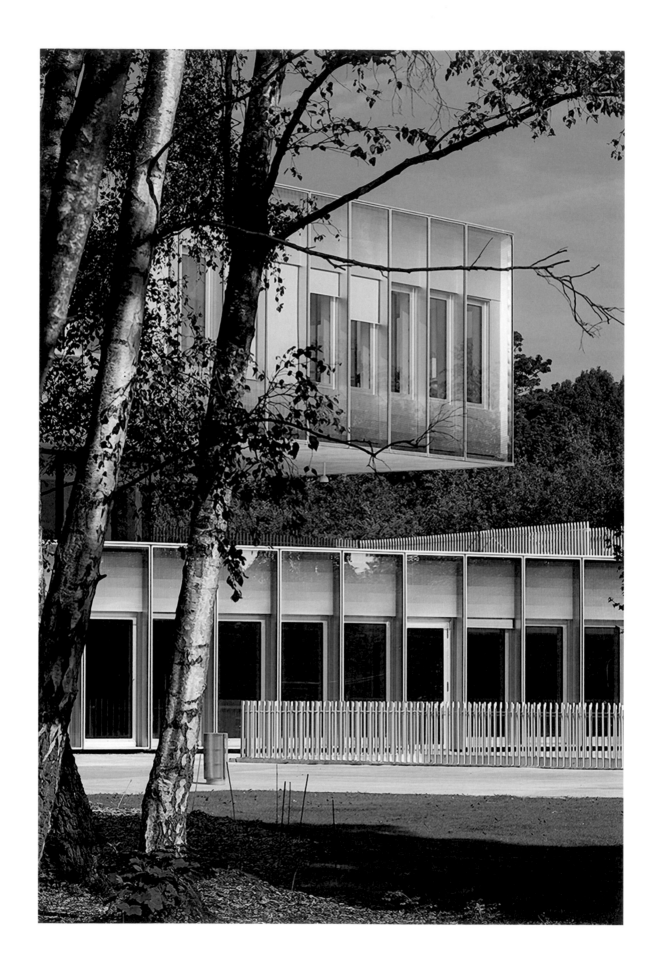

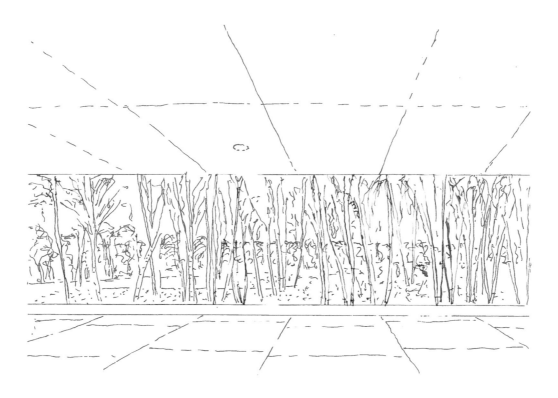

Symmetrically, the Chamber of Trades and Crafts is organized around six patios that provide natural light for most circulation spaces and divide the building into four clusters housing different realms and spanning through the whole three levels. Functions vary from local and regional administration to research and educational facilities (hairdressing school, cooking school, laboratories, classrooms).

The new building acts as a hub for both the Chamber and the associated training schools which had been previously scattered throughout the historic city centre of Lille.

IIn order to dialogue with the urban fabric and the surrounding landscape, the architects paid great attention to the use of natural materials: glass and stone. The ground and second floors are wrapped by a modular double glass façade that ensure climate control and quality acoustics. Spanning the full floor height, each module features an inner polished aluminum window which can be opened, and a fixed outer glass panel with a reflective print that gradually blends to create a fully transparent zone at eye level, while blending the building into nature.

Moreover, the patio façades, which feature large polished aluminum window frames, are clad in Vals Quartzite, a very solid, compact and frost-resistant stone from Switzerland. The same stone has been used on the patio floors.

Through its solid materiality, Eurartisanat aims to both articulate, absorb, and reflect the surrounding landscape while at the same time standing out as a new iconic element; an inhabited landscape dedicated to the public sphere.

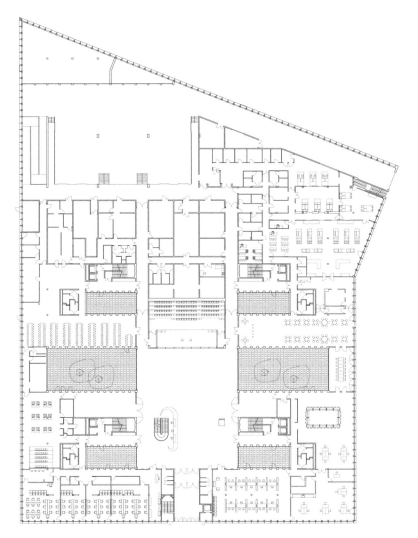

Ground Floor

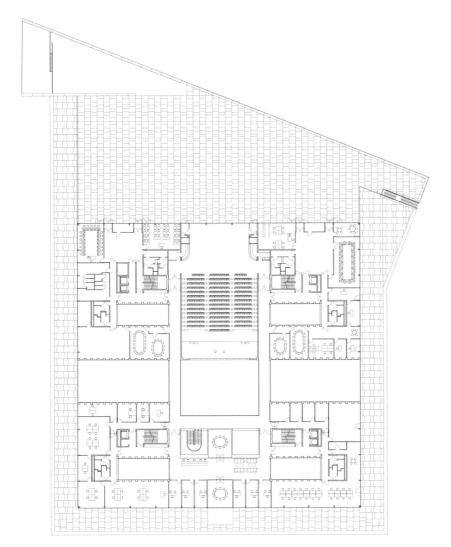

First Floor

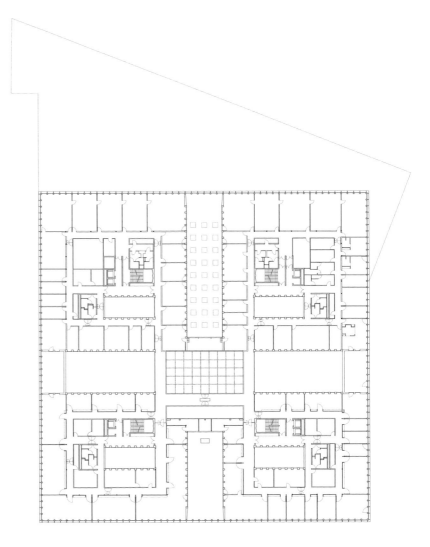

Second Floor

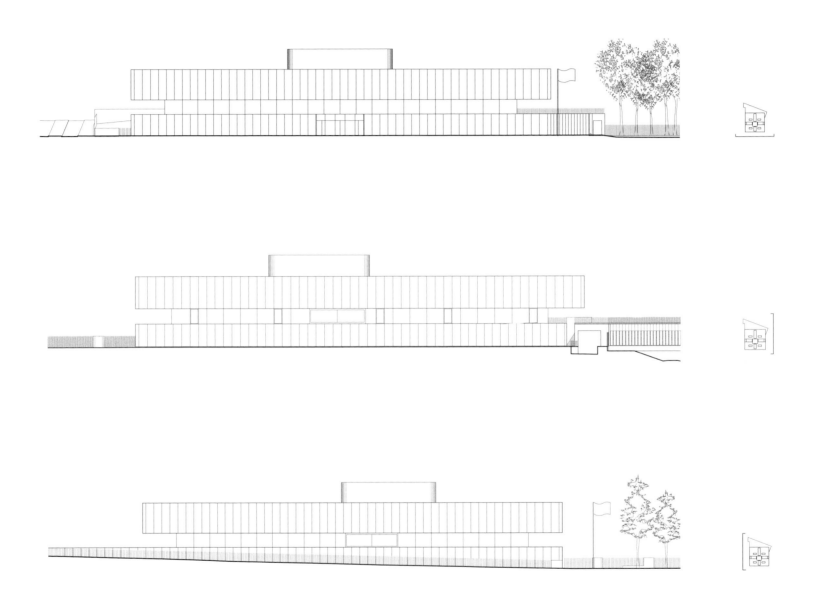

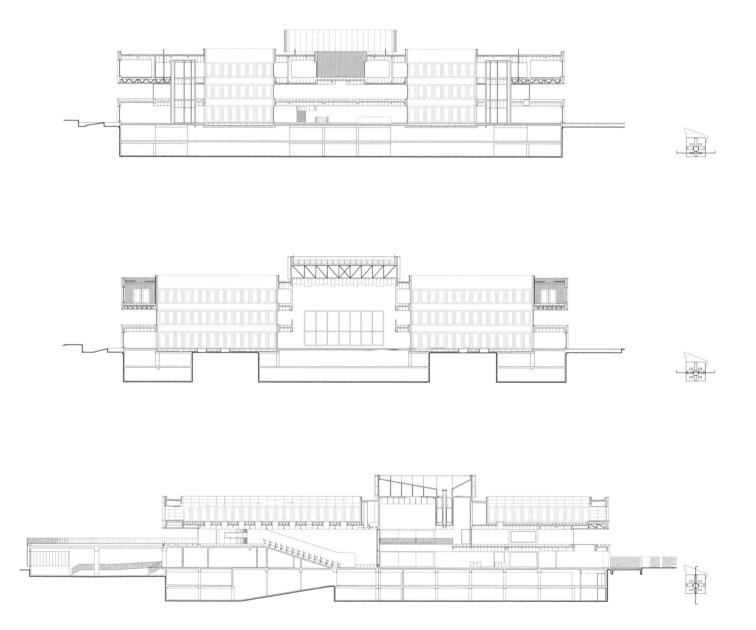

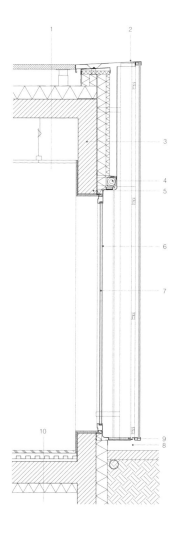

1. Roof Terrace
   - Prefab Concrete Panels on Adjustable Risers
   - Polyurethane Insulation
   - Concrete Slab
   - Suspended Ceiling
2. Polished Aluminium Cap
3. Façade (L-R)
   - Concrete Beam
   - Rock Wool Insulation
   - Aluminium Sheet
   - Single-glazed Silk Screen Printed Glass
4. Roller Blind
5. Painted MDF Panels
6. Polished Aluminium Window
7. Single-glazed Silk Screen Printed Glass
8. Ventilated Air Space
9. Polished Aluminium Sub-frame
10. Floor:
   - Stone or Resin
   - Heating Floor
   - Concrete Slab
   - Extruded Polystyrene Insulation
11. UPN Steel Profile
12. Painted MDF Panels

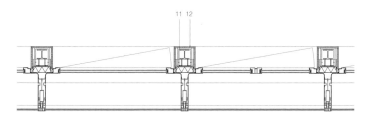

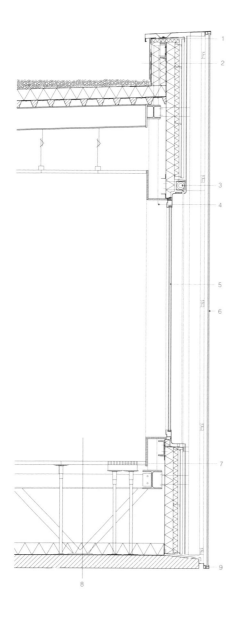

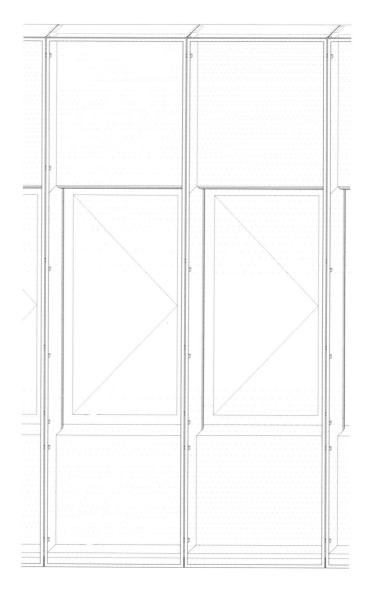

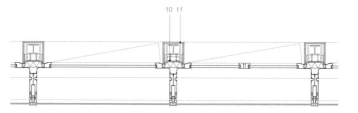

1.  Aluminium Cap
2.  Façade (L-R)
    - Metal Sheet
    - Metal Raised Edge
    - Rock Wool Insulation
3.  Roller Blind
4.  Painted MDF Panels
5.  Polished Aluminium Window
6.  Single-glazed Silk Screen Printed Glass
7.  Heating Gutter
8.  Floor:
    - Floor Panels on Adjustable Risers
    - Steel Truss
    - Glass Wool
    - Cantilevered Concrete Slab
9.  Ventilated Air Space
10. UPN Steel Profile
11. Painted MDF Panels

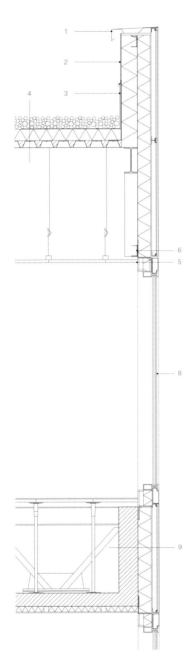

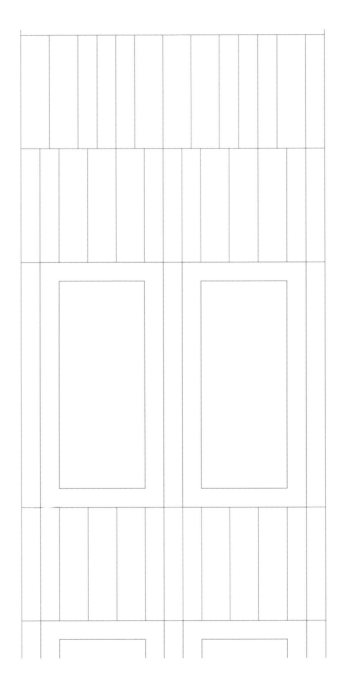

1. Covered Aluminium
2. Metal Sheet
3. Counter Flashing
4. Roof Terrace:
   - Gravel
   - Waterproofing
   - Polyurethane Insulation on
     Corrugated Metal Sheeting
5. Suspended Ceiling
6. Sub-frame
7. Flooring Panels on Adjustable Risers
8. Aluminium Double-glazed Window
9. Patio Façade (L-R)
   - Concrete Structure
   - Rock Wool Insulation
   - Supporting Structure/
     Ventilated Air Space
   - Vals Stone Cladding

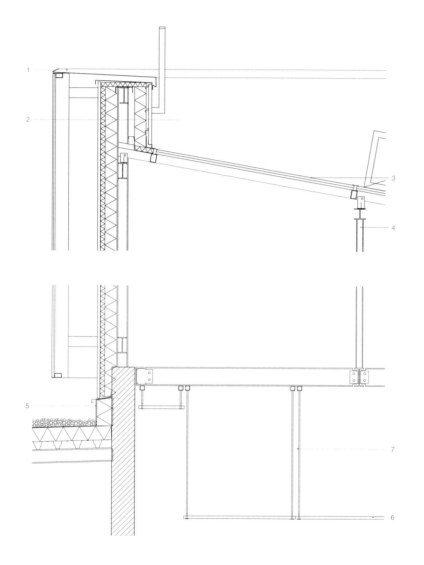
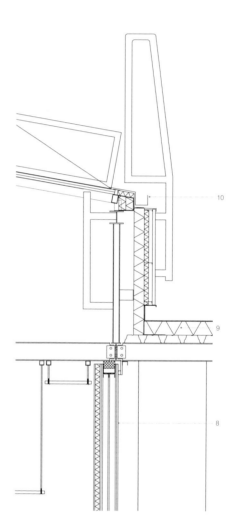

1. Aluminium
2. Wall:
   - Black Enameled Glass
   - Supporting Structure
   - Rock Wool Insulation
   - Metal Sheet
   - Rock Wool Insulation
   - Single Skin Metal Coating
3. Glass Roof
4. Steel Truss
5. Sealant
6. Opal Glass Suspended Ceiling
7. Threaded Steel Spindles
8. Acoustic Drywall
9. Polyurethane Insulation on Corrugated Metal Sheeting
10. Gutter

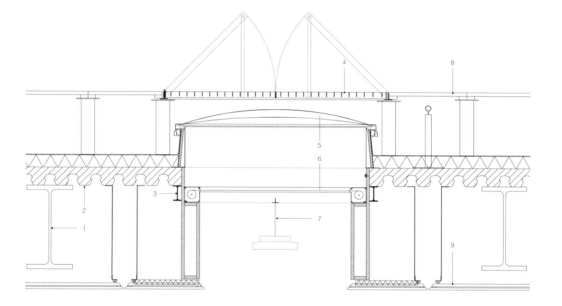

1. Main Steel Structure: IPE 550
2. Composite Floor on a Corrugated Metal Sheet
3. Secondary Steel Structure: IPE 100
4. Galvanized Steel Grating
5. Skylight With Polycarbonate Dome
6. Horizontal Roller Blind
7. Lamp
8. Wooden Floor Panels on Adjustable Risers
9. Suspended Acoustic Textile Ceiling (Kvadrat System)

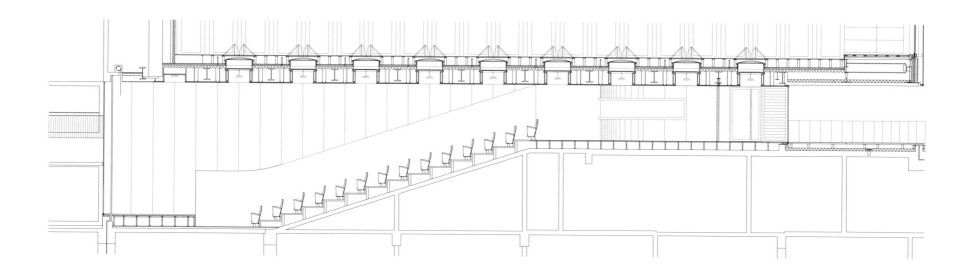

| 1 | | 2 |
|---|---|---|
| | 3 | |
| | 2 | |
| 4 | | |

1. Meeting Room: First Floor
2. Staircase to the First Floor
3. Open Corridor: First Floor
4. Office: First Floor

*"A great building must begin with the unmeasurable, must go through measurable means when it is being designed, and in the end must be unmeasurable."*
Louis Kahn

# URBAN ASSOCIATION

The main building, standing five stories tall, is positioned along the east-west tree-lined avenue. Its butterfly shape incorporates all the geometries related to the intersection of roads and public spaces. The presence of a tall and majestic tree in the middle of the site gives the building its configuration on a courtyard facing southwest. The north and south gable façades, which could receive what we can describe as the greatest "depth" of the urban landscape, therefore bend slightly under the effect of these perspectives.

The one-story houses are grouped together on the western part of the site. With dual orientations, they face north towards an allotment, and south towards a more urban courtyard. These houses are grouped together like a "horizontal plate" responding to the unity of the allotment gardens. A large and protected interior passageway, acting as a courtyard, serves as an entry point to all of these houses.

The two buildings are connected by a continuous concrete base, which echoes linearity of the old stone walls found in a sector of Nantes (known for its market gardening), examples of which remain in the southern part of the site.

The project houses mainly two-bedroom apartments (65 to 70 m$^2$); however, with the large variety of orientations that were possible, the intention was to unify the housing units around the principle of a unitary outdoor space; a loggia bringing more natural light to the main rooms (living room, kitchen, and bedroom) and onto the spaces would be extended visually.

This principle made it possible to identify an additional room for each apartment, approximately 2.50 m deep with, on average, 15 m$^2$ surface area. These particular spaces were treated in such a way so as to give privacy to each apartment, through an elaborate system of sliding shutters. This system brings protection not only from views in the public space but also from other loggias in the building or neighboring buildings, while simultaneously bringing depth and transparency to the façade.

Thus, this spatial expansion allows for the surrounding urban landscape to penetrate into the building, and allows for a multitude of uses that were observed and consolidated several months after the occupation of this building.

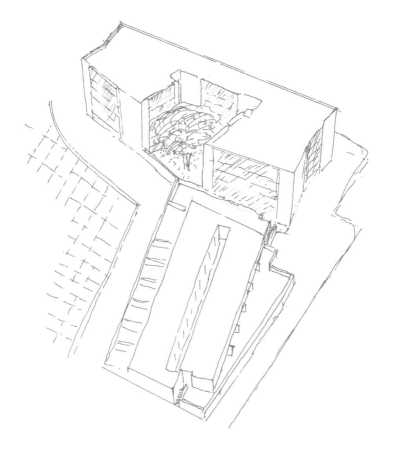

The individual houses grouped in duplexes are accessed from a private courtyard. They each benefit from a private garden.

Here again, the majority of typologies that are developed are two-bedrooms; however, these are supplemented on the first floor by an additional room of six to seven m² forming either a dressing room, a computer room, or a mini bedroom.

The architectural language of this project is directly issued from territorial, urban, and economic conditions as well as the values linked to "habitability" or how we live in our homes. Thus, the different façades respond to very distinct situations:
- The north façade presents a rather flat and regular urban elevation.
- In contrast, the seven other façades of this building look for a sculptural phenomenon winding around the site responding to the various surrounding urban landscapes.

The building for grouped individual housing is made up of a block placed on top of a concrete slab with completely glass façades for all of the living rooms. It is part of the overall horizontality of this part of the site, in relation to the allotment gardens and the tram line.

Resonance between the project and the different elements of the surrounding landscape and territory make it possible to obtain an architectural figure both anchored in a precise relationship to a site.

The project is carried out entirely in concrete left exposed or painted. The windows are built in aluminum fitted with canvas blinds. The openwork sliding shutters are made of lacquered aluminum tube. The project meets the thermal regulations in force within the framework of the Eco-quartier of Bottière-Chênaie (BBC – Effinergie).

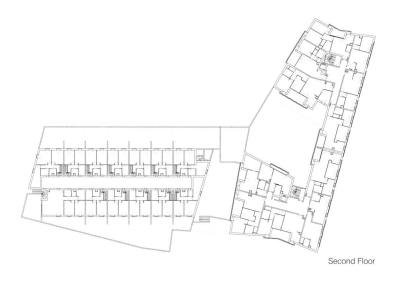

Second Floor

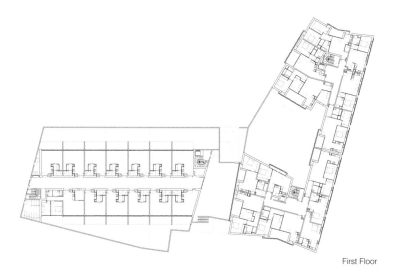

First Floor

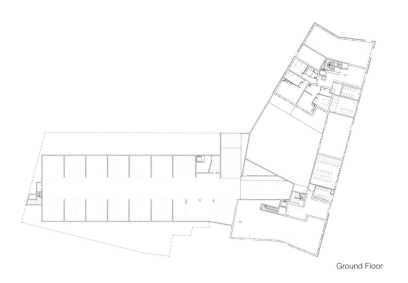

Ground Floor

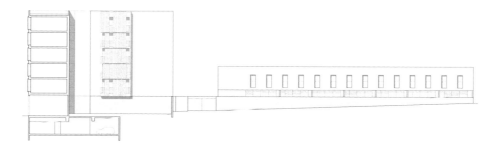

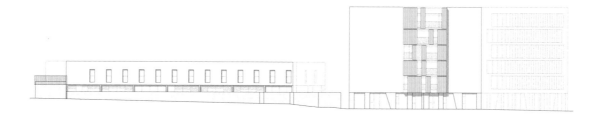

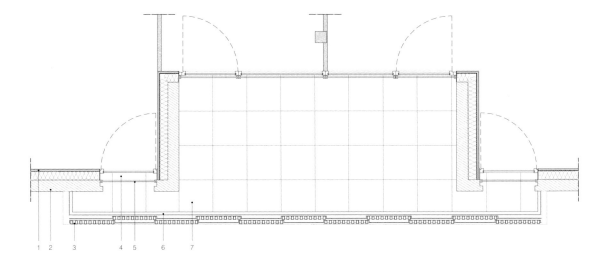

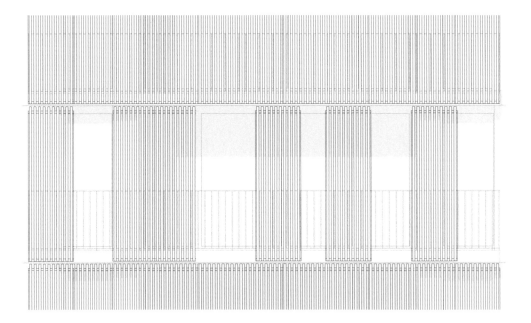

1. Polystryrene Insulation and
   Plasterboard
2. Concrete Wall
3. Aluminium Coated Steel Sliding
   Shutter
4. French Style Opening Coated
   Aluminium Sash
5. Roller Blinds Curtains
6. Galvanized Steel Balustrade
7. Slab on Blocks/Concrete 60 × 60 cm

# CONTEXT

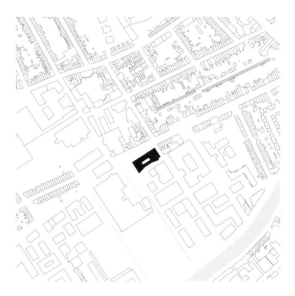

The building is located in a new district known as Rives de la Haute-Deûle, west of Lille city centre. Positioned between a residential area and an industrial zone, the building integrates these two different urban landscapes, providing a major transition.

The Rives de la Haute Deûle is one of the most important post-industrial districts and has been undergoing a transformation for 15 years. Its central project is the renovation of a textile factory rehabilitated as a innovative hub for IT companies, surrounded by urban development combining housing programs, offices, and public facilities as well as generous public spaces.

The first new office building, located along Avenue de Bretagne, links a residential area consisting mainly of historical workers' housing, and the large building of the former Leblan-Lafont factory, standing tall as if a great industrial castle. The tectonic quality of this construction has a strong presence within the site and was used as a focal point for all the surrounding projects, regardless of the materials used (brick or concrete).

The 6500 m² Bretagne office building was built using a certain geometry inspired by both the surrounding constructions and urban regulations.

Special attention was paid to defining the building's envelope and its tectonic qualities: load-bearing façades built using prefabricated, mass-tinted components, windows incorporating a large fixed structure, and an opaque aluminum panel.

These façade elements are found in all parts of the building, adapting to different situations and orientations of the surrounding landscape. The pleated molding of concrete alternates in different directions on each floor in order to create horizontal layers, reinforcing the urban transition between the smaller historical housing developments and the Leblan-Lafont factory. When inside the building, the window detail, with regards to its position to the horizontal slabs, gives great importance to framing the context and extending the feeling of the interior spaces towards the surrounding urban landscape.

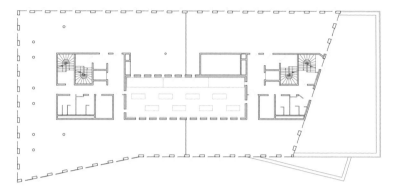

Second Floor

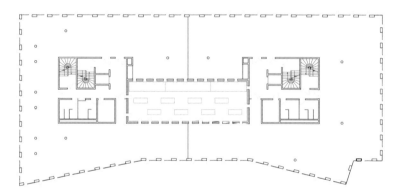

First Floor

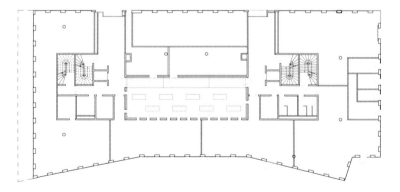

Ground Floor

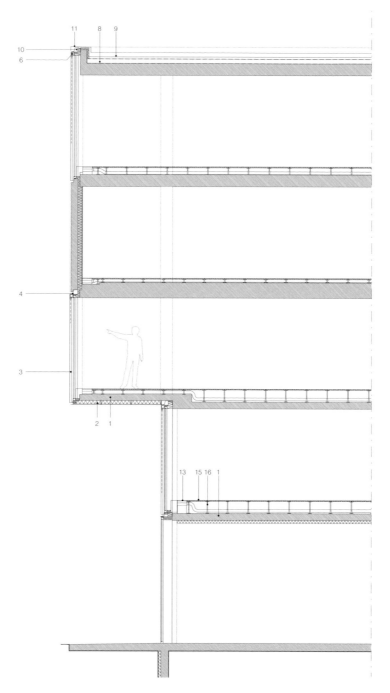

1. Concrete Slab
2. Thermal Break Insulation
3. Coated Aluminium Sash
4. Coated Aluminium Hood
5. Galvanized Steel Bracket
6. Roller Blinds Curtain
7. Coated Aluminium Hood for Blinds
8. Insulation 20 cm
9. Elastomer Sealing
10. Angle Fixing
11. Coated Aluminium Cover
12. Heating Board Cover
13. Blow-molding Stainless-steel Grill
14. Retarder
15. Slab on Blocks
16. Adjustable Fixing for Slab on Blocks

West Façade Section

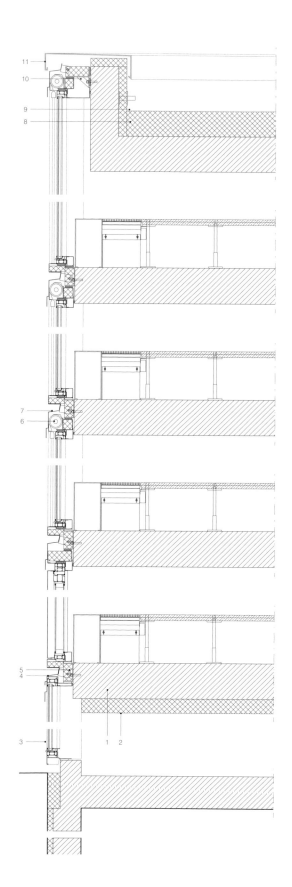

1. Concrete Slab
2. Thermal Break Insulation
3. Coated Aluminium Sash
4. Coated Aluminium Hood
5. Galvanized Steel Bracket
6. Roller Blinds Curtain
7. Coated Aluminium Hood for Blinds
8. Insulation 20 cm
9. Elastomer Sealing
10. Angle Fixing
11. Coated Aluminium Cover

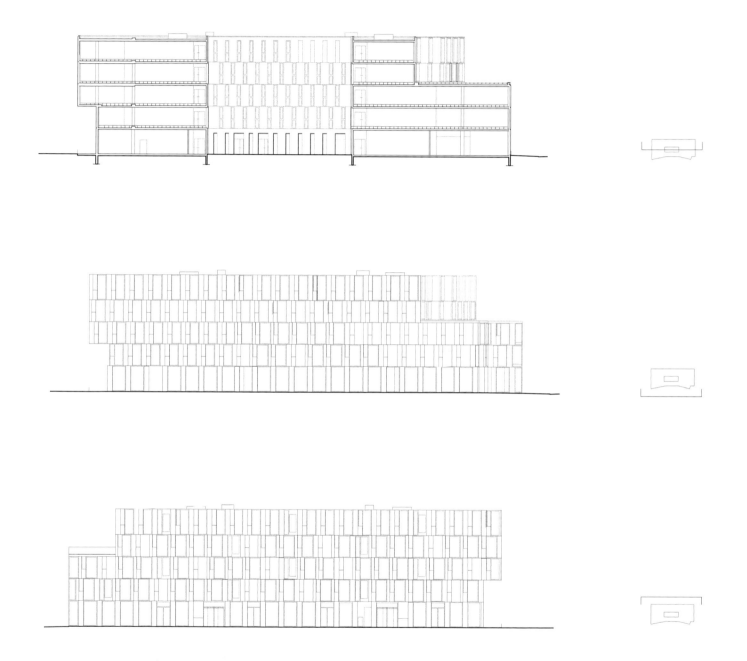

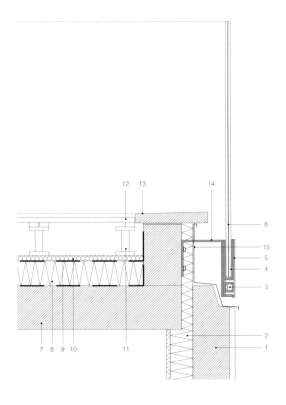

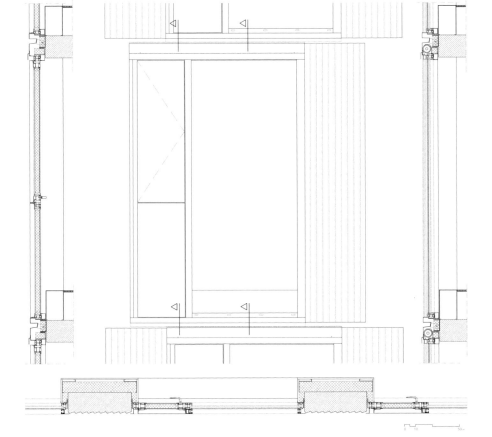

1. Precast Concrete Element Grey
   Anthracite
2. Plaster Board Insulation
3. Metal Tube 50 × 50
4. Plate 200 × 10
5. Aluminium Coated Sheet
6. Glass Sheet 44-2
7. Concrete Slab
8. Polystyrene Insulation
9. Elastomer Sealing
10. Rigid Insulation
11. Timber Structure
12. Timber Board
13. Converted Precast Concrete
14. Steel Profile

*"Of course you condition perception through a building but you must be careful not to overdo it, otherwise you asphyxiate the user. It is necessary to find the right balance between the control of the experience of space, and a freedom which allows things to happen."*

Alvaro Siza

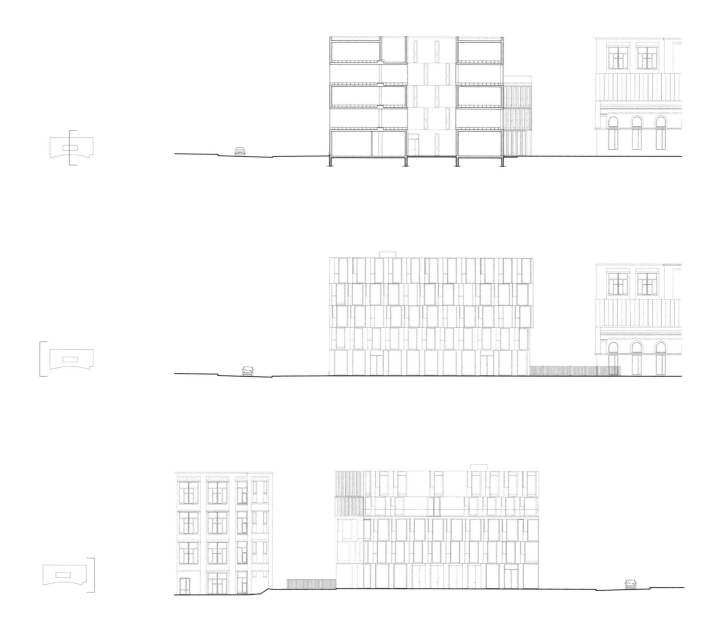

# TECTONIC

This building is located in the new Bottière Chênaie neighborhood in eastern Nantes. Its trapezoidal shape reflects the planned contours of the neighborhood.

Exemplary construction techniques were a key factor in the conception of this project as the building is to be used by students of various building trades. Thus, architectural tectonics was an issue of major cultural significance. A long-span wood beam structure is used (40 m), with concealed metal support systems. The impression of floating, with unraised structural efforts, characterizes the spatiality of the workshop's large surface.

The façades are built entirely with wood (Douglas and Eucalyptus for the windows).

The building occupies two levels:
- On the ground floor, the main hall opens directly onto the large workshop and the teachers' room. An outdoor workshop sheltered by a broad awning serves as an extension to the indoor workshop.
- One flight up, the four classrooms and changing rooms are accessed by a long corridor looking out onto the workshop below.

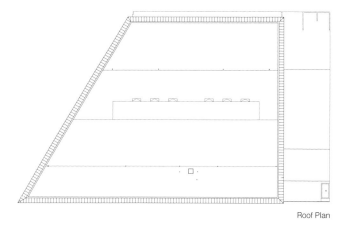

Roof Plan

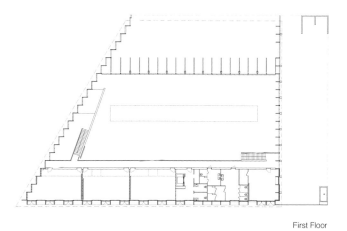

First Floor

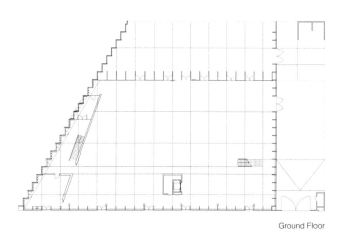

Ground Floor

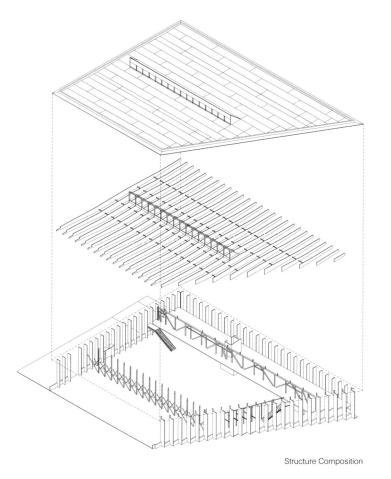

Structure Composition

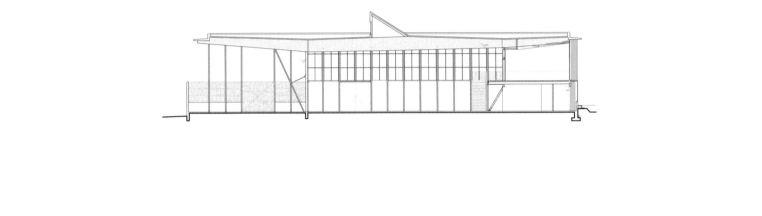

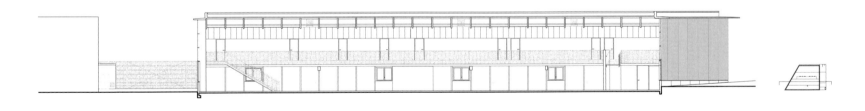

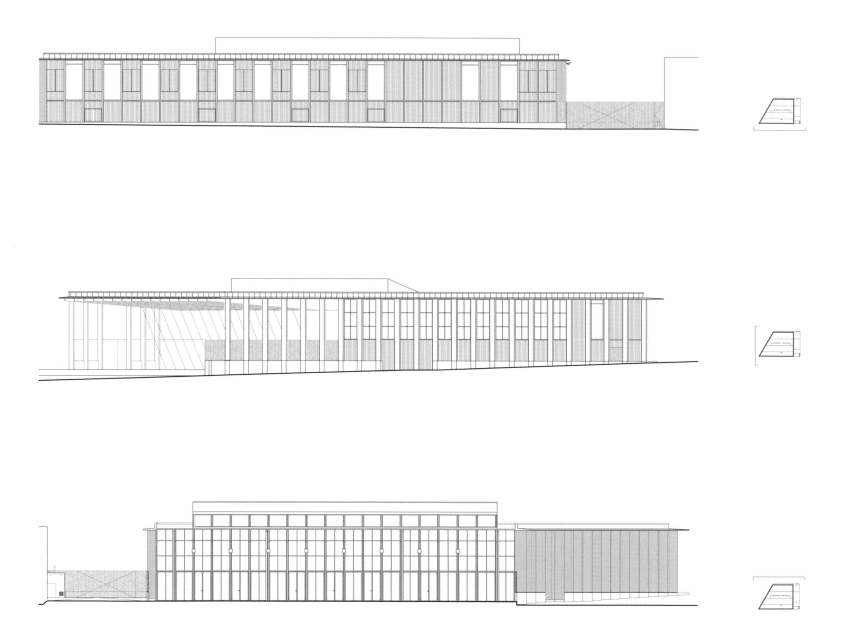

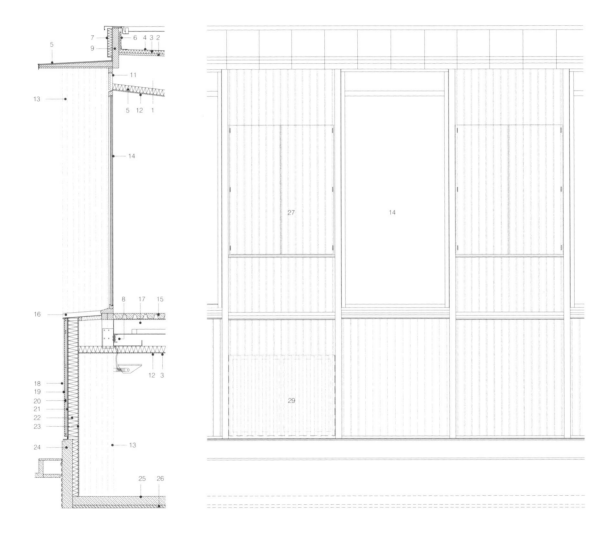

1. Laminated Stuck Beam
2. Kerto Panel
3. Insulation
4. Waterproofing
5. Standing Seam Zinc Quartz Cover
6. 12/10 mm Galvanized Skylight Frame
7. Standing Seam Zinc Quartz Cladding
8. UPN 140
9. Laminated Stuck Edge Beam
10. Douglas BLC
11. Wooden Transom
12. Placoplatre Suspended Ceiling
13. Laminated Stuck Wooden Column
14. Fixed Sash
15. Concrete Floor Topping
16. Aluminium Headguard
17. IPE 270
18. 19 mm Thick Vertical Strip Cladding
19. 22 × 45 Counter-needling and Needling
20. Waterproofing
21. 9 mm Triply
22. Wooden Framing + 145 Insulation
23. 12 mm Pyroply
24. Concrete Base
25. Concrete Surface Slab
26. Balast
27. Opening Sash
28. HEA 240
29. Timber Batten Cladding

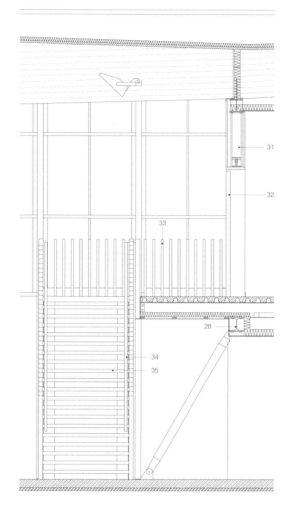
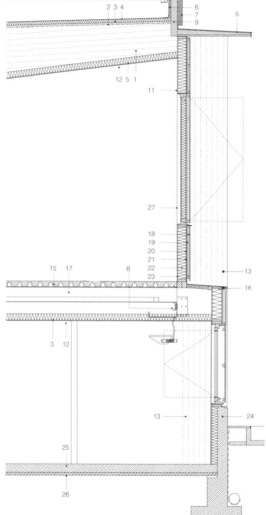

1. Laminated Stuck Beam
2. Kerto Panel
3. Insulation
4. Waterproofing
5. Standing Seam Zinc Quartz Cover
6. 12/10 mm Galvanized Skylight Frame
7. Standing Seam Zinc Quartz Cladding
8. UPN 140
9. Laminated Stuck Edge Beam
10. Douglas BLC
11. Wooden Transom
12. Placoplatre Suspended Ceiling
13. Laminated Stuck Wooden Column
14. Fixed Sash
15. Concrete Floor Topping
16. Aluminium Headguard
17. IPE 270
18. 19 mm Thick Vertical Strip Cladding
19. 22 × 45 Counter-needling/Needling
20. Waterproofing
21. 9 mm Triply
22. Wooden Fframing + 145 insulation
23. 12 mm Pyroply
24. Concrete Base
25. Concrete Surface Slab
26. Ballast
27. Opening Sash
28. HEA 240
29. Timber Batten Cladding
30. Window
31. Danpalon Louvre
32. Classroom Door
33. Metal Tube 100 × 40 mm
34. Wooden Handrail Diam 50 mm
35. Metal Plate Stair Step 330 × 1320 mm
36. HEA 200

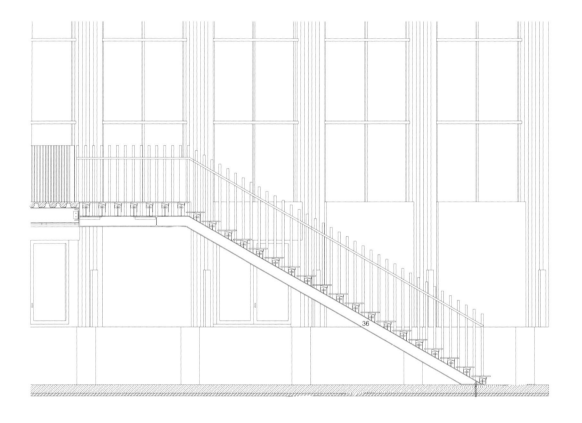

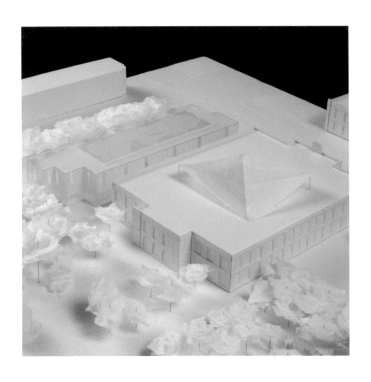

# MEMORY AND CREATION

The Exposition park site has undergone many transformations since the 19th century and has recently been granted Metropolitan Park status. Nevertheless, these successive alterations have created much confusion in the interpretation of this utilized space. Our proposal is to revive the Park based on a six-item guideline:

- Revealing historical outlines through the design of a uniting monument and rebuilding an identity by showcasing the existing historical pavilions.
- Redefining the edge of the forest in order to protect the park from the street.
- Prioritizing pedestrian traffic flow and access routes, mainly with the creation of a new shaded pathway that would run from the lower gallery of the new building and alongside Garcilaso de la Vega Avenue. This promenade would extend along the entire length of the Metropolitan Museum. The open-air parking will be enhanced as a garden pergola.
- Offering a large esplanade on the western part of the new building, which in turn widens the existing sidewalk on Garcilaso de la Vega Avenue.
- Reconnecting the park with its geographical context through the presence of water running from north to south; a refreshing element within this public space.
- Replanting the entire grounds by associating both native plants and introducing new species, thus enhancing the biodiversity of the Park.

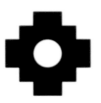

Chakana:
Federative Figure

Central Clearing
Vegetal and Water Volute

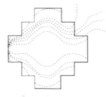

Forest Edge

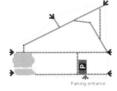

Main Walkways

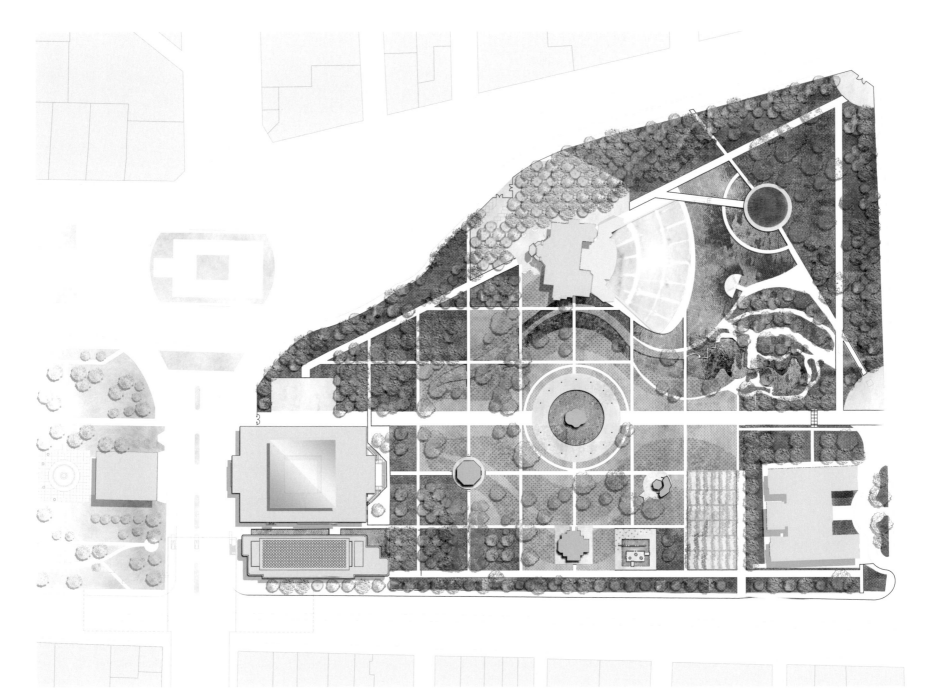

The new wing of the MALI is positioned on the northwest corner of the site, at the junction between Garcilaso de la Vega Avenue and 9 de Diciembre Avenue, both of which are dominated by car traffic.

Both for urban and programmatic reasons, we suggested creating a new pavilion in the Park of the Exposition that would address this two-fold challenge. Seeking to redefine the urban landscape, it would offer high-quality places for a wide range of future visitors.

The building consists of three levels with exactly the same proportions as the current MALI building. The new building is roughly 10 meters away from the existing building.

The program is clearly organized spreading out over three levels. On the ground floor is the entrance, the library, the restaurant, and the archives.

The first floor is entirely dedicated to the educational dimension of the Institution and the second floor hosts the exhibition halls.

On the lower floor, an urban gallery runs alongside the avenue, with a metro exit on the north end, that gives access to the south, to the central hall, but also to the restaurant and its terrace in the park, or to the library. All of these access points can operate autonomously.

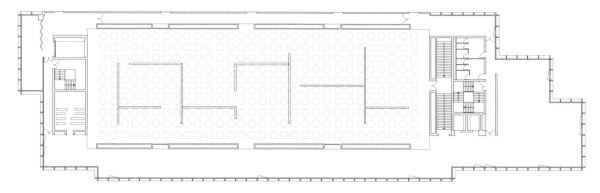

Second Floor

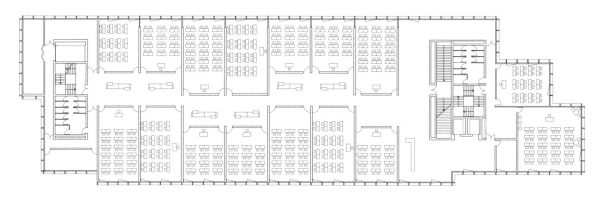

First Floor

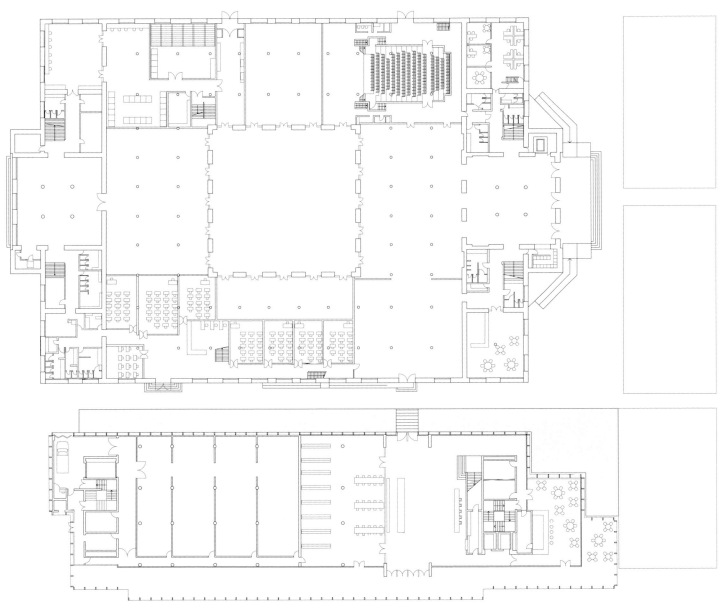

Ground Floor

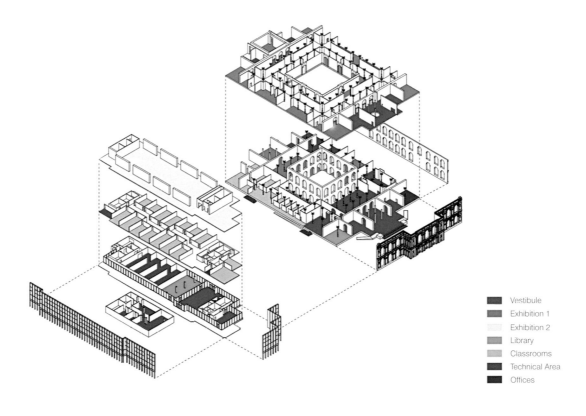

| | |
|---|---|
| ■ | Vestibule |
| ■ | Exhibition 1 |
| □ | Exhibition 2 |
| ■ | Library |
| ■ | Classrooms |
| ■ | Technical Area |
| ■ | Offices |

A second entrance to this museum wing is provided through the sculpture garden, which acts as the new development between the old building and the new one. In this entrance hall, a large staircase leads up to the first floor, which opens onto all of the classrooms.

The classrooms are bathed in natural light, as are the reception and waiting areas. Contemporary museums have a particular connection to light. Artworks can only be presented by putting this fundamental element to use in the architecture.

The exhibition halls consist of three units, a large surface area of nearly 1,200 m$^2$ with no load-bearing posts. This allows for high flexibility in organizing exhibitions. This large space is equipped with a highly-controlled radiant light device that unifies the environment of this museum space. A gallery along the western façade provides access to the exhibitions and offers long walls on which the art can be displayed.

Finally, a more intimate exhibition hall towards the park. It can be used to exhibit singular artworks such as sculptures (if so desired) and feature openings onto the landscape.

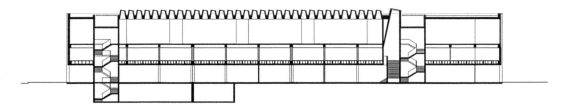

Longitudinal Section

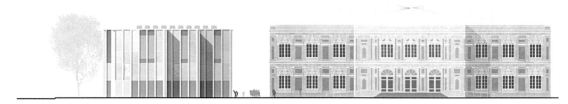

South Elevation

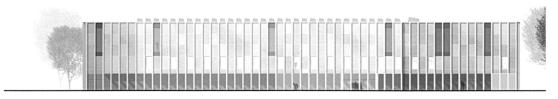

South Elevation

# RESONANCE

This project for 17 apartments in Pantin (north of Paris) is part of a general renovation project which has been underway for several years, led by the town council for the center of Pantin. The project addresses one of the major questions that has arisen in France over the past few years: the gradual reduction of housing surfaces guided by economic interests that today govern housing production.

Whereas social housing has been a powerhouse for innovation in housing forms throughout the 20th century, privatization has largely reduced innovative options for exploring different ways of living. The spaces extending the apartments, such as terraces, loggias, and patios, constitute a possibility of innovation while opening up the living spaces. Protected outdoor spaces, as a theme, are developed here in a suburban context with high-traffic streets. To deal with this situation, a certain resonance appears on the façade between different architectural styles found in and around the site, and the project, with its balconies and terraces which are otherwise completely absent in the neighborhood.

The double façade therefore allows for better intimacy using polycarbonate shutters, while providing outdoor spaces for each apartment in the residence. This housing program is organized around a central courtyard, with a staircase and elevator for all levels as a central nucleus. Wood façades and windows appear in these outside spaces.

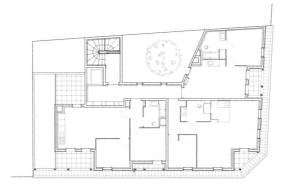

Second Floor

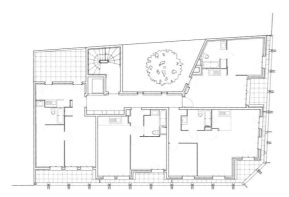

First Floor

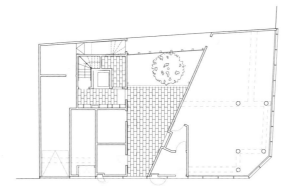

Ground Floor

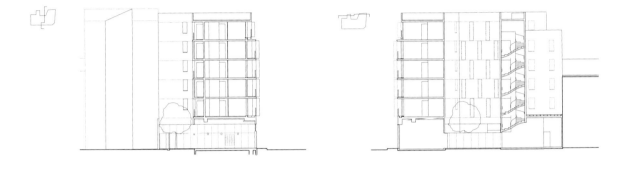

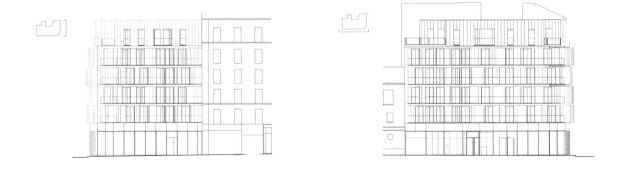

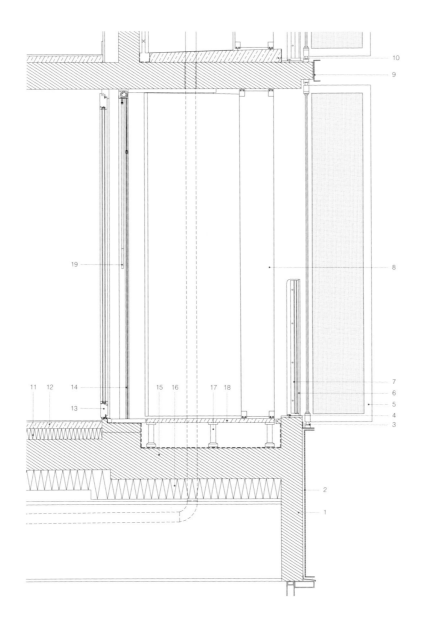

1. Concrete Wall
2. Aluminium Coated Metal Cladding
3. Coated Steel $30 \times 50$mm
4. Platinum Fixation $150 \times 50$ mm
5. Polycarbonate Shutter and Aluminum Coated U Profile $50 \times 50$ mm
6. Coated Steel Structure:
   - T Profile $50 \times 50 \times 10$ mm
   - L Profile $20 \times 20$ mm
7. Glass Sheet
8. Glass Separation
9. Aluminium Coated Cladding Profile
10. Concrete Screed
11. Polystyrene Insulation 50 mm
12. Concrete Screed
13. Wood Sash
14. Aluminium Blind Rail
15. Concrete Slab
16. Polystyrene Insulation 100 mm
17. Steel Block
18. Concrete Panel $50 \times 50$ cm
19. Roller Blind Curtain

# SCALE AND DIVERSITY

The renovation of the Cité du Pavé Blanc, an area of primarily social housing on the edge of the Meudon Forest West of Paris, consists of rehabilitating pre-existing buildings on site (800 apartments), redesigning public space, and the construction of 84 new housing units. Accompanied by the creation of a new tram station, this renovation project participates in a larger urban reintegration and requalification of the neighborhood.

The surrounding housing estates from the 1960s/1970s have all the characteristics for being completely independent from the neighboring urban and landscaped contexts, with tower and linear buildings constituting the dominant model.

The first phase made it possible to build four- to five-story housing ensembles, giving a more urban scale opposite the tram station and allowing a gradual urban transition.

The different buildings are built around a central nucleus with a staircase and lift, giving out onto two to three apartments per level.

Great attention was paid to the orientation and lighting of many rooms, including the bathrooms. The loggias protected by metal blinds with adjustable slats offer a high-quality exterior extension to these living spaces.

The building is constructed using prefabricated white concrete walls for façades, called "pré-mur" using a double-panel of concrete with isolation in the middle. The ground floor, acting as a base for the building, is built in stone, which in turn masks the parking lot on the ground floor and acts as a sustainable and long-term quality material visible to passersby.

Second Floor

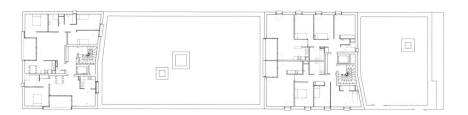

First Floor

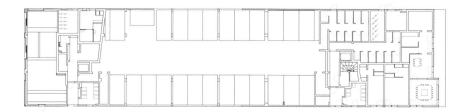

Ground Floor

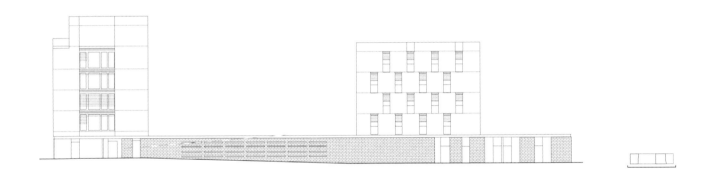

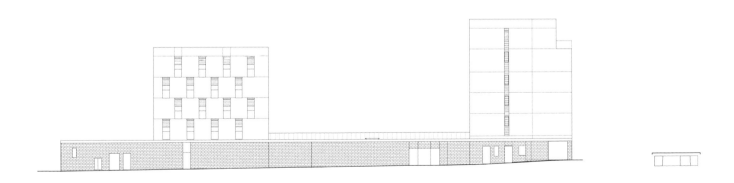

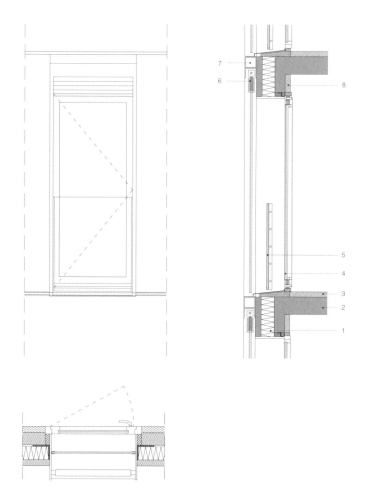

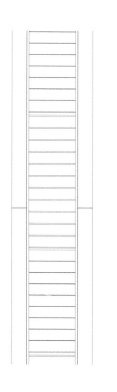

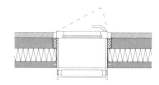

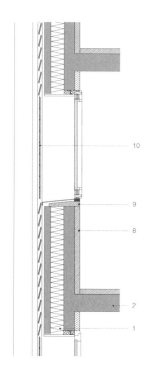

1. Wall Element, White Concrete:
   - 7 cm Exterior Concrete
   - 15 cm Insulation
   - 13 cm Interior Concrete
   - Plaster Board 50 mm
2. Concrete Slab 20 cm
3. Concrete Screed 50 mm
4. French-style Opening
   Aluminium Sash
5. Glass Balustrade, Fixed with
   Steel Brackets
6. Louvre Blind
7. Steel Tube 100 × 100 mm
8. Plaster Board
9. Concrete Window Sill
10. Plantation Shutters

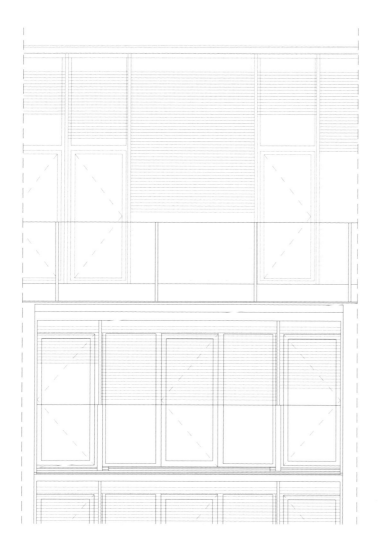

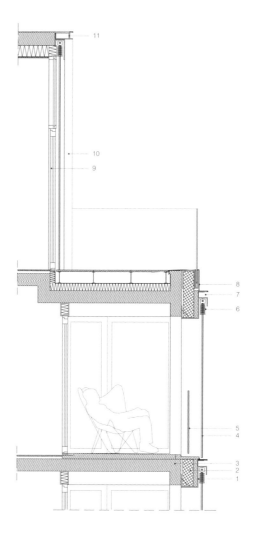

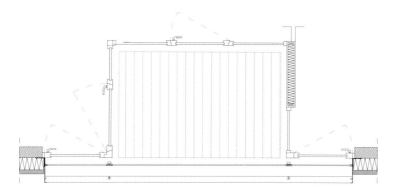

1. White Concrete Panel
2. Insulation 100 mm
3. Concrete Slab
4. Blind Rail
5. Glass Balustrade, Steel Coated Metal Brackets
6. Louvre Blinds
7. Coated U Metal Profile 100 × 100 mm
8. Balustrade:
   - Metal Profile 300 mm
   - Coated Cladding
   - Glass Sheet 44.2
9. White Coated Aluminium Sash
10. Metal Tube 50 × 30 mm
11. Coated Steel Profile:
    - Tube 150 × 50 mm
    - U 50 × 30 mm

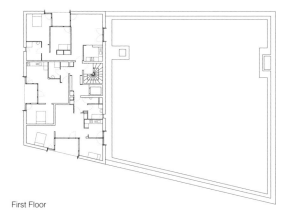

First Floor

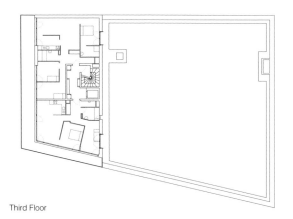

Third Floor

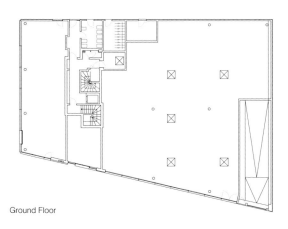

Ground Floor

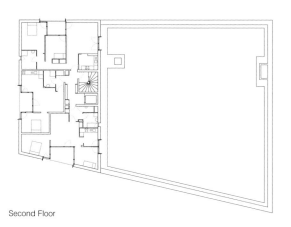

Second Floor

# STRATIFICATION

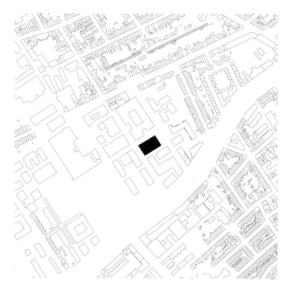

The "Black Diamond" building is located in the new district of the Haute Deûle in Lille and is emblematic for this site due to its mixed-use program. The Haute Deûle - Euratechnologie project is one of the main urban developments of the city of Lille, bringing together IT companies, housing projects, public facilities, and many public spaces, combining new designs with pre-existing post-industrial buildings that have been recently renovated and transformed into housing and offices. Taking back this urban site meant simultaneously responding to the need for creating a lively and sustainable new district, as well as ensuring the future economic and metropolitan development of the zone through the creation of a space dedicated to digital technology.

Stratification in this part of the city lies at the heart of the reflection for this architectural concept. Programmatic diversity is the structuring element creating the dynamics for this neighborhood. The "Black Diamond" building is the perfect illustration for this strategy, occupying the full plot with its 200-parking-lot silo, a sports facility, and office spaces, with access to the east square for one of the two entry points. The car park is spread over seven half-levels (two of which are semi-underground); one level is accessed by the west side. The sports facility is located on the third floor. The fourth and fifth floors are office spaces organized around a central patio that serves as a common area accessible to all employees.

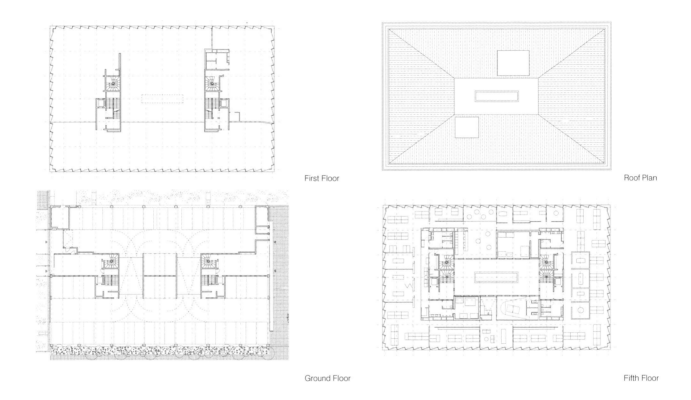

First Floor

Roof Plan

Ground Floor

Fifth Floor

In relation to the urban landscape and the association of programs, the choice of a strong expression resulted in the use of contrasting materials. Thus, the parking levels are surrounded by a red brick wall with an elaborate moucharaby. This latticework design filters light into the car park, giving a pleasant atmosphere. Black lacquered metal windows are used in the façade for the upper levels.

The large sets of office windows are broken down into a fixed glass panel and a shutter opening for individual natural ventilation. The sloping roof completes the volume, covered with a dark seal. The structure of the car park consists of pre-manufactured concrete, the three upper floors of a metal structure. Two halls, west and east, provide easy access to the building. They are treated with large plates with marbled patterns to expand a space of 2.26 m high. Within the framework of this project, the layout of the offices on the fifth floor offers transparencies, allowing light to circulate naturally.

On this same floor, a large elegant dining room and a mini-basketball court provide relaxation and escape from the corporate environment. So, this project proposes to combine two major ambitions. The first is to innovate in the association of very different programs by creating an exemplary micro-urbanity for the whole of this district. The second is to assume the industrial and cultural heritage of this post-industrial territory and to reveal its poetic dimension.

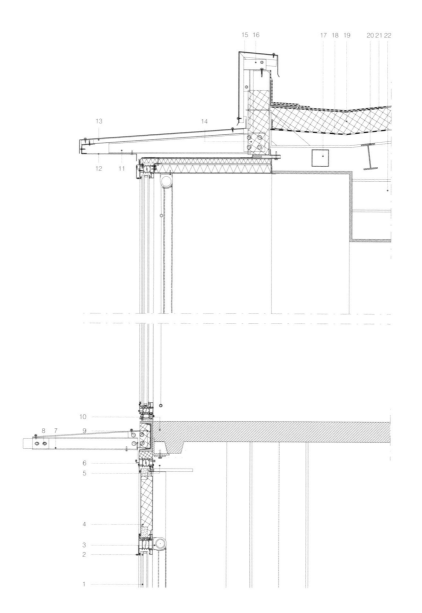

1. Polished Aluminum Sash
2. Aluminum Profile for Thermal Break
3. Roller Blinds Curtains
4. Sandwich Panel:
   Insulation + Polished Aluminum Sheets
5. L Profile, Fixing Sash 50 × 50 mm
6. Fixing Plate 50 × 50 mm
7. Metal Console H 50 × 120 mm
8. Coated Steel Sheet
9. U Steel Profile 140 × 80mm
10. Corrugated Steel Deck Structure
11. Metal Console
12. Coated Aluminum Cladding
13. Coated Aluminum Cover
14. Steel Fixing Plate 60 × 60 mm
15. Coated Aluminum Cover
16. Fixing Plate, L Steel Profile
17. Tube 80 × 80 mm
18. Seal
19. Insulation 20 cm
20. I Profile 120 mm
21. PVC Membrane
22. H Steel Profile Structure 200 mm

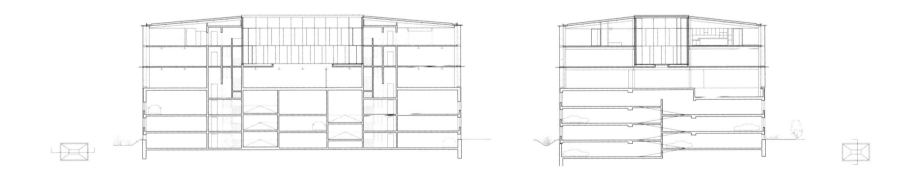

179

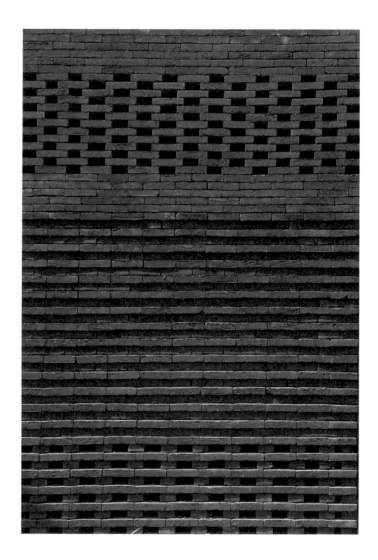

*"The sun never knew how great it was until it hit the side of a building."*

Louis Kahn

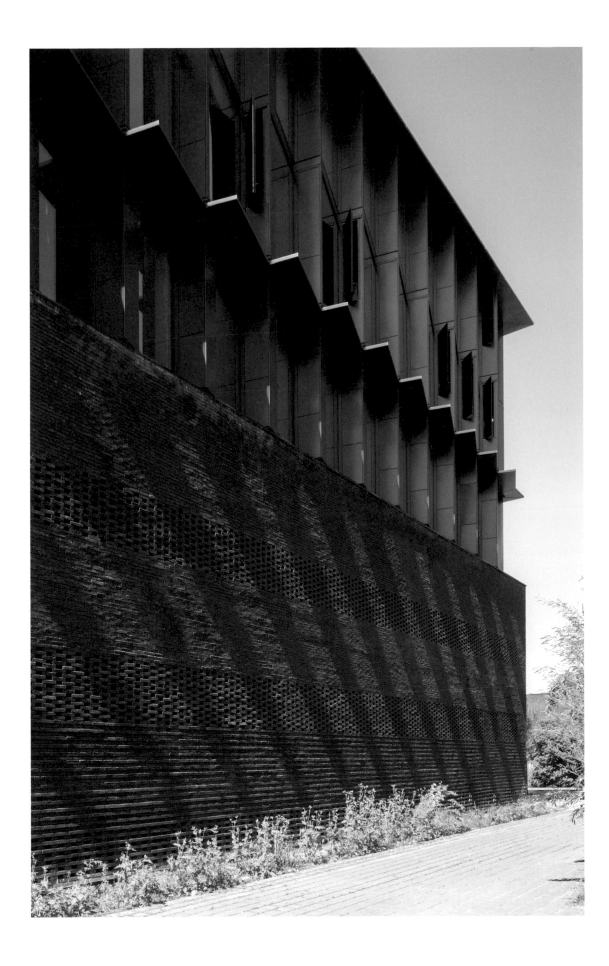

# NEW IDENTITY

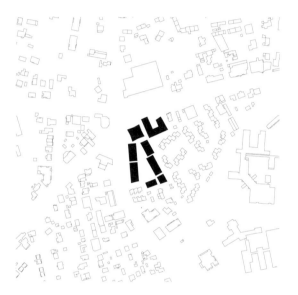

The project is based on reflections at a territorial scale and a precise site analysis. The first objective was to provide comfortable quality spaces, protected from nearby traffic, and to develop a peaceful space at the heart of the project.

The buildings are organized around major landscaped areas: a wooded meadow and an evergreen garden, inspired by the "secret garden" north of the site.

Around this first landscape, the different programs span out into eight different buildings, all very open towards this generous space. Around the garden, where existing trees have flourished, the main housing program was developed. Along the major tramline, we chose to set back the buildings in order to create more public space in line with the commercial occupation of the ground floors and the tramway station. Inside the block, as part of the general organization of the project within this 150 m site, we chose to create pedestrian pathways on the eastern and southern edges, each of which would connect to the adjoining avenues, Avenue Pasteur and Avenue du Haut-Lévêque. The pathways give access to all the housing ensembles and are carefully designed using porous paving stones to mitigate the sealing of the land.

The open block, as mentioned, is porous and offers a series of passages and visual transparencies between the avenues and the wooded meadow at the heart of the project.

These passages provide access to the main halls of each building as well as to the service areas. A large gap between the two main buildings on the Avenue du Haut-Lévêque offers, at one point, a wider opening onto the meadow. Likewise, the quieter interior paths can be used to reach the tram station from Avenue Pasteur.

Collective Housing

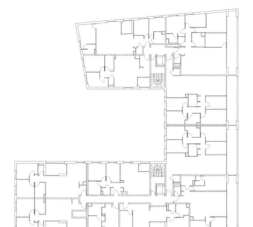

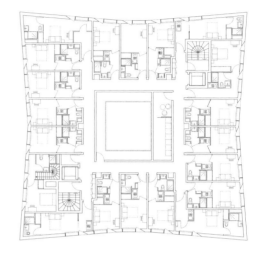

Hotel

First Floor

First Floor

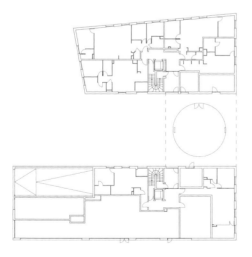

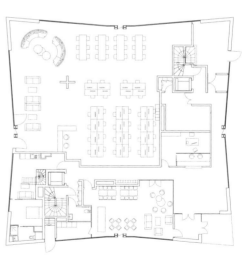

Ground Floor

Ground Floor

Collective Housing

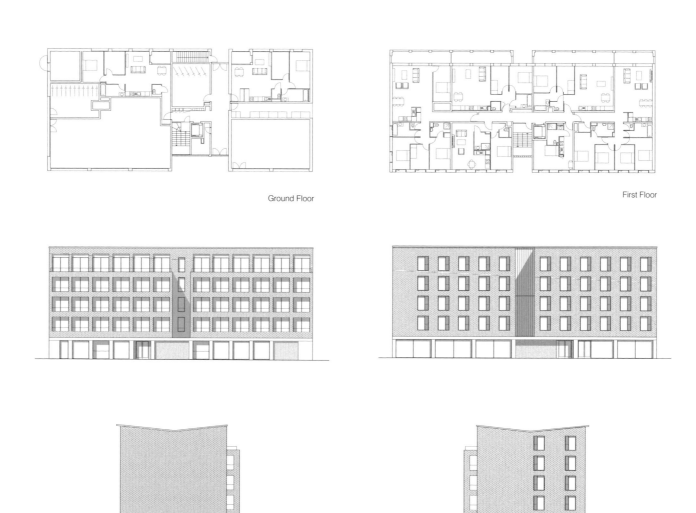

Ground Floor

First Floor

Multi-family Housing

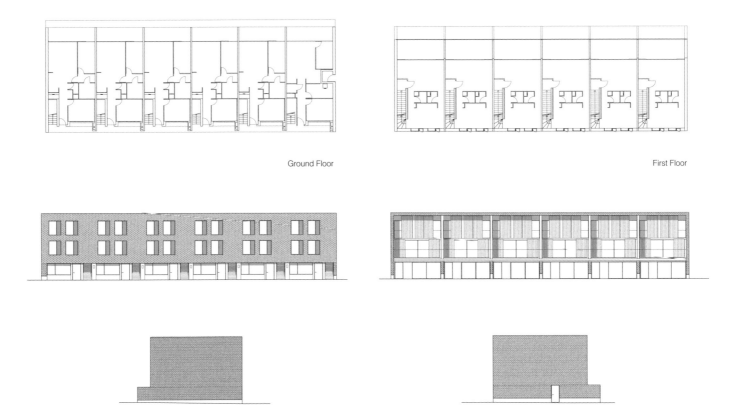

Ground Floor

First Floor

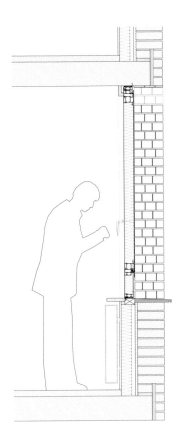
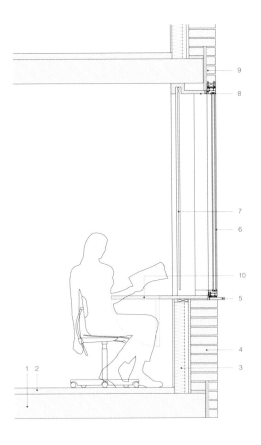

1. Concrete Slab
2. Concrete Screed
   + Thin Floor Covering
3. Insulation 8 cm
4. Maxi Brick 22 × 22 cm
5. Stone Sill
6. Coated Aluminum Sash
   - Fixed Window 150 × 170 cm
   - Opening With Window Sill
     60 × 150 cm
7. Interior Curtain
8. Wood Cover
9. Brick Mortar + Insulation
10. Folding Shelf

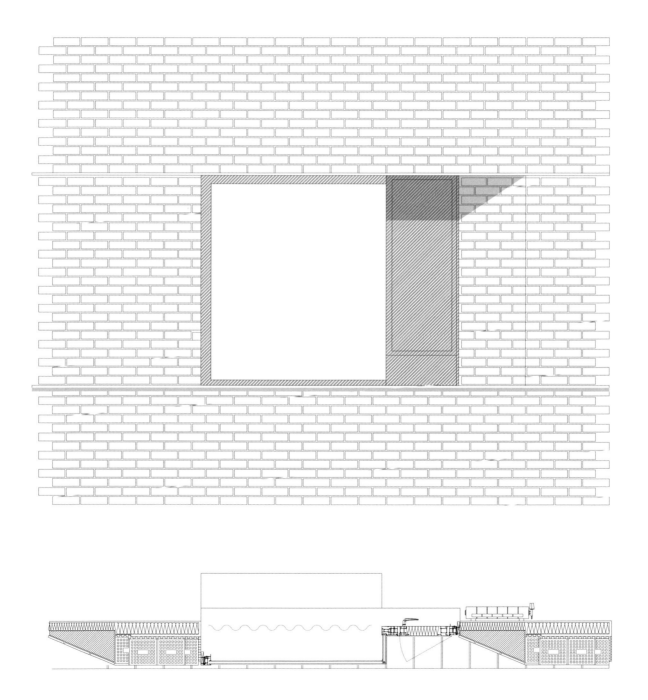

# SUSTAINABLE TERRITORY

# ENVIRONMENTAL REPARATION IN WESTERN CHINA: THE YUZHONG SETTLEMENT

Kenneth Frampton

The proposal for the future ecological development of an expanding rural community is the most critically creative comprehensive project the architect has worked on to date. Invited in 2019 to participate in a multi-disciplinary design team in partnership with the Centre Scientifique et Technique du Bâtiment (CSTB), Pranlas-Descours has been responsible for not only imagining a new ecological interface between urbanization and agriculture for Yuzhong but also evolving a new kind of residential unit capable through its specific form of improving the ecological and productive capacity of the region. In addition, as far as is feasible, the overall project is designed to restore the region's original climate. Environmental degradation in Yuzhong results from wanton clear-cutting of trees on the high ground to the south of the settlement and, as is the case elsewhere, over-taxing the aquifer. In this regard, the project envisages the extremely ambitious strategy of restoring the natural hydraulic capacity of the entire site, first, by a systematic tree-planting on the range of hills to the south of the settlement, and second, by the installation of a series of concrete storage tanks, which are in effect honey-combed reservoirs designed for the filtration and storage of rainwater. According to the CSTB, this sequence of strategically placed tanks has the capacity to generate one million cubic meters of water per annum, with the flow entering the settlement via four main canals in order to feed into a network of irrigation channels and eventually replenish the water of the Nanhe River which bounds the settlement to the north.

The reforestation of the adjacent high ground to the south intends not only to shade the environment in order to compensate for the extremely high temperature of the region in summer but also to create localized humidity and induce cloud formation and hence precipitation which, admittedly, under the circumstances, is a relatively long-term project in which rainwater collection will provide the most immediate benefit.

The ultimate strategy for the housing interventions is to introduce a "finger plan," comprising six medium-rise planned developments of varying size into the existing valley settlement, wherein bands of interstitial agriculture alternate with built fabric. Needless to say, this proposal has to be flexible enough to accommodate the existing fragmentary agricultural pattern, consisting of villages along with clusters of houses. One of the primary tasks of the architect was to design a new residential typology capable through its specific form of augmenting the ecological food-producing capacity of the region.

This complex intention combined with densifying the population is the basis of the residential prototype, namely a five-story perimeter block, accommodating four, four-bedroom and two, two-bedroom units per floor, arranged around a central court for three consecutive floors, with agricultural storage on the ground floor and greenhouse cultivation on the top floor. This uppermost floor is articulated in such a way as to combine plantings with solar panels and a means for collecting rainwater. The photovoltaic panels are intended to generate an autonomous electrical energy system, divided between the production of light and the provision of hot water. Finally, the construction of this generic residential unit has also been conceived to minimize embodied energy through load-bearing walls built of thick, prefabricated adobe blocks, in effect a modernized version of traditional French "pisé" construction combined with glulam timber beams supporting secondary rafters and board floors of timber.

Photo of the Nanhe River of Yuzhong, China

The overall ecological strategy is predicated on recycling and composting household waste, which, compounded with livestock manure, will produce biogas and fertilizer. Apart from collecting rainwater, provisions will also be made for the storage and reuse of gray water within the household system. At the same time, due to the prevailing high temperatures of the region in summer, the main canals are to be

Alvar Aalto, Master Plan of Imatra, Finland (1946)

covered with boardwalks so as to minimize the loss of water through evaporation. This new medium-rise, high-density residential pattern will be served by public transport, beginning with its link to the high-speed, trans-continental rail system being built throughout China. A single primary east-west transit system will extend from a high-speed terminal through the valley settlement to serve north-south bus and bicycle routes running up through the plan towards the river along with transverse branches in accordance with the Chinese government's ecological policy of minimizing the use of private cars. The primary east-west light rail system will bend up towards the north in order to connect to the regional city of Lanzhou.

Aside from the highly sophisticated, montaged perspectives featuring the future public life of this urbanized rural community, one of the most beautiful renderings by the architect is the detailed master plan showing the future Yuzhong. With exceptional precision, the image shows existing random conglomerations of built fabric, varying in density and interlaced with the six north-south strips of new, urbanized development that vary somewhat in terms of both size and orthogonal consistency; the village nearest to the high-speed rail terminal has the most well-ordered street pattern. Apart from this initial village, nothing could be further from the *tabula rasa* of the modern planning tradition than the way in which every intervening village has been inflected to accommodate and integrate the existing residential fabric. In this regard, the master plan could hardly be more organic and realistic, betraying a connotation to Alvar Aalto's highly mosaic plan for Imatra in Finland dating from 1946.

In Pranlas-Descours' master plan, as with Aalto's Imatra plan, old and new are treated as if they are part of the same living organism. As the architect puts it: "The main ambition of this project is to work within the human conditions of this landscape with a new form of sustainable urbanization. We want to integrate these villages and the agriculture in an urban proposal that does not destroy the history of the place through developing a new water system of irrigation which resolves the question and is in keeping with the earth's natural resilience."

Through its pattern of land settlement, this eco-city development posits the idea of a mutually beneficial, dynamic interaction between agriculture and urbanization. This type of reciprocal condition is in contrast to the suburbanizing tendency of the time-honored Anglo-American garden city tradition that dominated much of the last century. Further, the condition is in opposition to the apocalyptic policy of the Chinese government from 1986 to the millennium, which drastically reduced in the space of 30 years the agrarian population of the country from 70 million to a figure of 2.5 million, entailing the loss of villages at a rate of 300 villages per day, which accompanied a mass migration of the populace into dense, treeless, high-rise megacities.

Kenneth Frampton

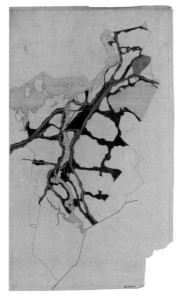

This policy, which contradicted Karl Marx and Frederick Engels' Communist Manifesto of 1848 advocating the dispersal of existing urban populations over the countryside, has recently been reversed by the government, which is now seeking the physical restoration and economic revitalization of regional agrarian settlements throughout China. In this regard, it is hardly an accident that the local government would commission the Yuzhong project in 2018 as part of the larger national policy of rural revitalization. However, as opposed to the touristic, cultural emphasis evident in much of China's rural revitalization, this project envisages a totally symbiotic sustainable integration between urbanization and agricultural production. One senses that the deeper, even polemical, significance of this work resides in its implicitly critical and creative reaction to the emerging depletion of water resources along with the equally threatening loss of available land through non-sustainable, megalopolitan suburbanization. Herein lies its unique epoch-making character, namely, its formulation, for the first time in the past century at least, of an ecologically viable and sustainable pattern of land settlement.

The Integrated Landscape of Yuzhong

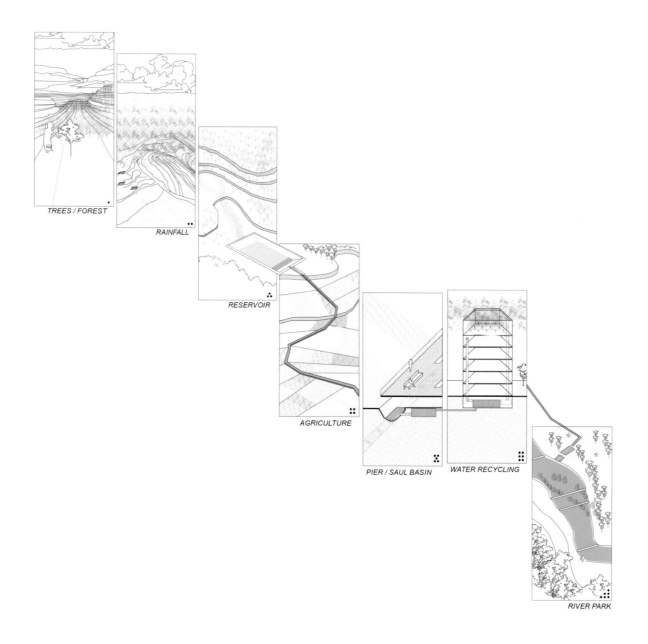

TREES / FOREST

RAINFALL

RESERVOIR

AGRICULTURE

PIER / SAUL BASIN

WATER RECYCLING

RIVER PARK

# A TALE OF WATER

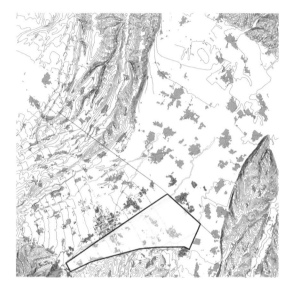

"Climate change" is one of the main questions for our future.

For the past 30 years, we have been the passive spectators of the earth's degradation. One of the planet's biggest challenges today is water. So many present-day phenomena and natural disasters display how rising water levels have the power to destroy and damage territories and their populations.

At the same time, there is the question of dehydration. In an opposite evolution of ground aridification, we have drained the wells dry: lakes are disappearing, rivers are drying up and people are parched and dying.

In West China, in the arid region of Gansu, for the District of Yuzhong we propose a reverse strategy for restoring a certain climate while maintaining the population within the original landscape through an extensive urbanization project.

For several years, this district in the part of the City of Lanzhou has been engaged in a great urban territorial project.

This specific site on which we have established a proposal is, from many aspects, emblematic of the typical and also incredible landscape of West China.

In this huge territory alongside the Nanhe river, urbanization is present through different modes of settlement. For a very long time, farming villages have occupied this site and have organized the landscape through their extensive activities. However, north of the river, a new densification has emerged and is in stark contrast to the farmers' villages.

From the river to the hills in the south, a large agriculture territory is under pressure of heavy urbanization. The agricultural activity therefore has to resolve the water question in order to survive, offering new models of sustainable agriculture.

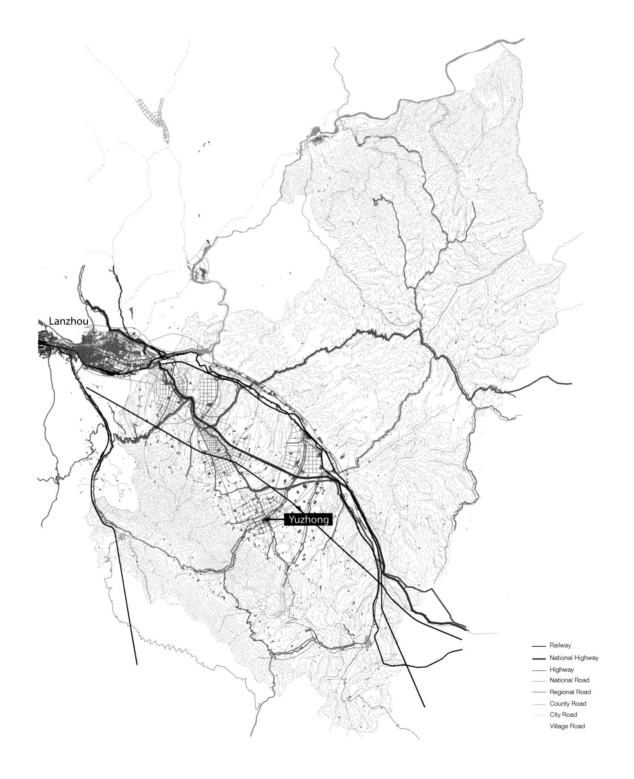

Lanzhou

Yuzhong

Railway
National Highway
Highway
National Road
Regional Road
County Road
City Road
Village Road

The main ambition of the project is to work within the human conditions and limitations of this landscape with a new model of sustainable urbanization. With our partner, the CSTB, we want to integrate these villages and the agriculture in an urban proposal that does not destroy the history of the place, by redeveloping a new water system for irrigation, which resolves the question and is in keeping with the earth's natural resilience.

The model is like a finger plan, which begins in the hills along the Nanhe river, where large lands of alternative agriculture are in relation with housing and social programs in continuity with the old villages.

To organize this strategy, we propose to use the traditional agricultural greenhouse.

The foundation of our strategy is to create a new model of six metropolitan villages, which will integrate all the ancient villages.

The urban and landscape strategy is to work directly on soil quality and water capacity. The soil is considered as a social, economic and political question. This Climate Restoration Project aims to demonstrate that with techniques and intelligence we can invert the gradual deterioration of the earth.

The six metropolitan villages are organized around a main street with a new typology of housing mixed with commerce. On the east and the west, there is a housing typology with greenhouses on the top, and terraced housing north of the river. East, around the new railway station, a mixed program with offices and housing will be developed.

PUBLIC SPACE OF TRADITIONAL VILLAGES

URBAN LIFE ON THE COVERED CANAL

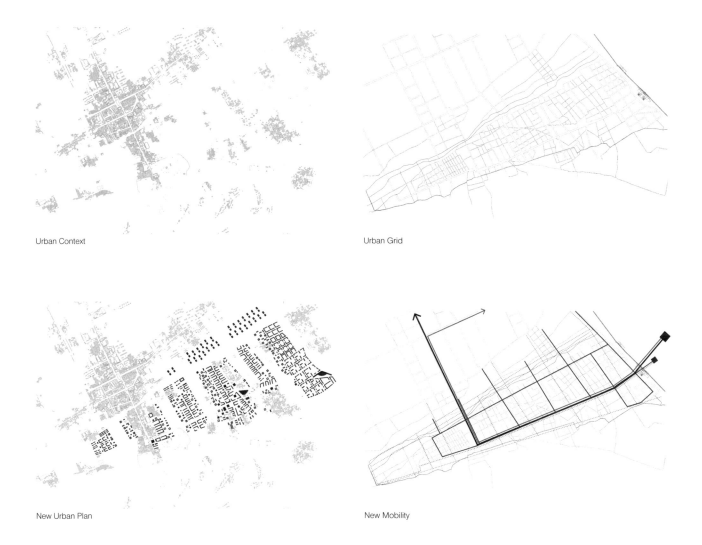

Urban Context

Urban Grid

New Urban Plan

New Mobility

Topography

Conserved Agriculture

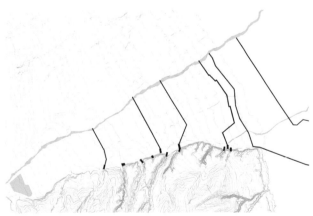

Water Connection

Integrated Landscape

**MASTER PLAN**
**Yuzhong County, Lanzhou**

LEGEND

| | Water |
| | Covered Canal |
| | ULHS Resevoirs |
| | Urban Green Space |
| | Conserved Agriculture |
| | Urban Agriculture |
| | Exisitng Agriculture |
| | Projected Building |
| | Existing Building |

0    0.1   0.2        0.4KM

## HYDROSYSTEM

Water is a crucial issue for this territory and is essential for the maintenance of the population and agricultural activity, particularly with a densification process. In this part of West China, the evaporation of water is a very complex question.

The urban and landscape strategy focuses on soil quality. We proposed the following interventions:
- planting a forest on the hill in the south which reduces the temperature and increases the formation of clouds and rainfall
- capturing the water from the hills by a series of filter blocks upstream which will be held in storage tanks
- developing basins to collect and store filtrated water
- covering south-north canals with a series of long pedestrian promenades to the Nanhe river
- obtaining a total stored water volume of 1 000 000 m³/year
- using complementary water by catching the rainwater on the roof of each building, and also transforming domestic water consumption patterns

The soil is a vital issue of social, economic and political importance. The "Climate Restoration Project" wants to demonstrate that with techniques and intelligence we can reverse the earth's degradation process.

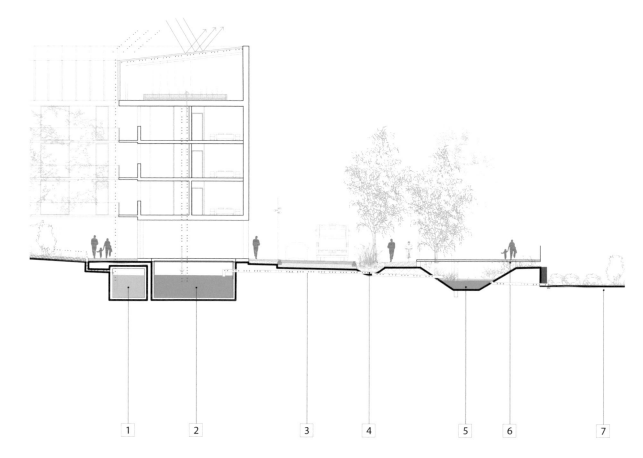

1 Rainwater Collection
2 Gray Water Collection
3 Drainage Pipe
4 Infiltration Vegetation Band
5 Canal
6 Wooden Pier
7 Agricultural Land

**LEGEND**

River

Stream Water

Existing Drainage

Urban Drainage

Agricultural Drainage

USHL Reservoir

Project Canal

Rebuild Canal

0  0.1  0.2  0.4KM

## AGRICULTURE

This project pursues a dual objective:
- strengthening the presence and development of agriculture with a hydraulic strategy
- renewing agricultural practices according to several traditional methods, as well as innovative cultivation

These ambitions require articulating production systems by creating associations between all modes of residential integration and activity. By creating a sequence of compost recoveries, transfer of energy related to buildings, gray water recycling, etc., we are offering a sequential system that demonstrates its sustainability without creating any oppositional forces between densification and agricultural landscape. This productive agricultural strategy is directly dependent on urbanization and this urbanization needs proximity to agriculture to constitute a stable and generative ecosystem.

Different cultivating systems are available: natural soil, traditional greenhouse, soil-less cultivation, or vegetable gardens linked to homes. Each of these cultivating methods makes it possible to offer a wide variety of production in the six categories of culture for Yuzhong: cereal crops, cash crops, forage crops, ornamental plants, trees and fruits, tobacco or green fertilizer.

This ambitious project aims to fortify and renew the traditional, social, and cultural history of Chinese society.

Agro-urban Cycle

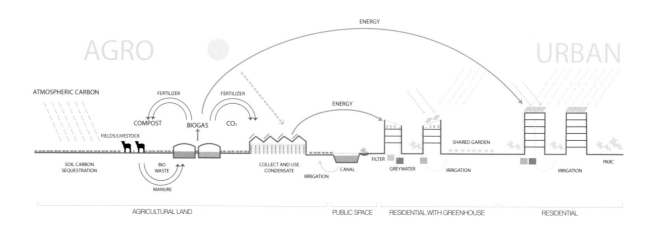

Agro-urban Exchange

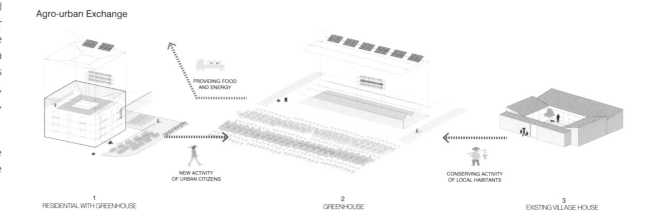

1
RESIDENTIAL WITH GREENHOUSE

2
GREENHOUSE

3
EXISTING VILLAGE HOUSE

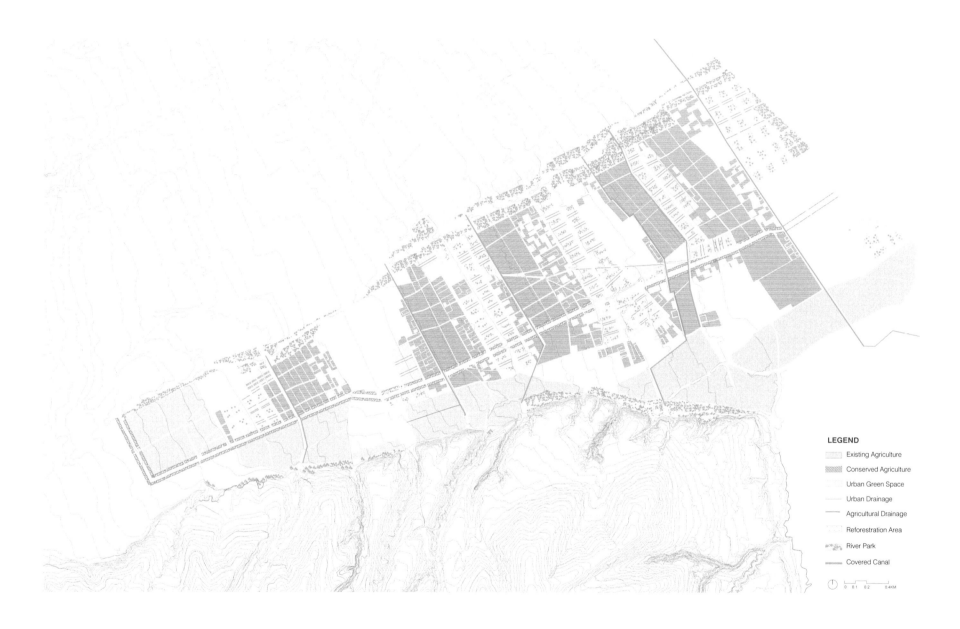

**LEGEND**

Existing Agriculture

Conserved Agriculture

Urban Green Space

Urban Drainage

Agricultural Drainage

Reforestration Area

River Park

Covered Canal

0  0.1  0.2        0.4KM

## HABITAT

For many years, Chinese urbanization has destroyed many old villages in the course of densification. In the Yuzhong project, between the Nanhe River and the hills in the south, a large agricultural valley is occupied by a series of villages. This project proposes to conserve this traditional urban implantation and at the same time to redevelop a more sustainable agriculture program, an essential foundation for maintaining the local population. The urbanization process began with a specific analysis of the human installation.

The model is a finger plan which begins on the Nanhe river to the hills with large land segments of alternative agriculture in relation to housing and social programs in continuity with the old villages.

The foundation of our strategy is to create a new model of six metropolitan villages integrating all the villages, which proposes a specific typology of new residential buildings. These new constructions develop an articulation between the agricultural fields with more classic housings of eight levels. New housing types bring together three levels housing units with a basement for agricultural storage underneath, and a greenhouse on the top floor. These mixed-use buildings offer comfortable apartments for peasant families who work directly on the fields.

These residential buildings will use traditional earth construction with brick around the courtyards. The greenhouses use the same traditional technique that we find in the fields: earth walls for heat conservation during the night. These constructions integrate the global urban strategy to reduce energy consumption.

Traditional Housing Plans
Different Organizations with the Courtyard

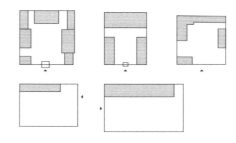

Traditional Rammed Earth House
with Timber Structure

1 Rammed Earth Wall
2 Stone Base
3 Wood Pad
4 Wood Beam
5 Supporting Column
6 Wood Deck

New Scale, New Typologies

TYPE 1

Six-story Residential
Building with Courtyard

RAIN WATER COLLECTION
SOLAR PANELS
WASTE COMPOST

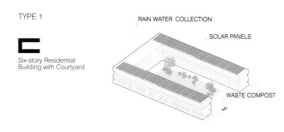

TYPE 2

Four-storey Residential
Building with Greenhouse

URBAN FARMS FOR LOCALS
GREYWATER COLLECTION
WASTE COMPOST
BIOMASS PRODUCTION

TYPE 3

Nine-story Residential
Building with Terraces

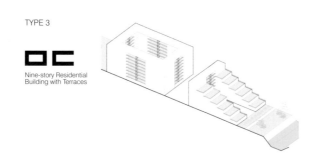

TYPE 4

Mixed-use Business
Block Office Towers
with Residential
Buildings

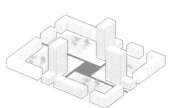

LEGEND

■ Projected Building

■ Greenhouse
Residential

▨ Existing Building

0   0.1   0.2      0.4km

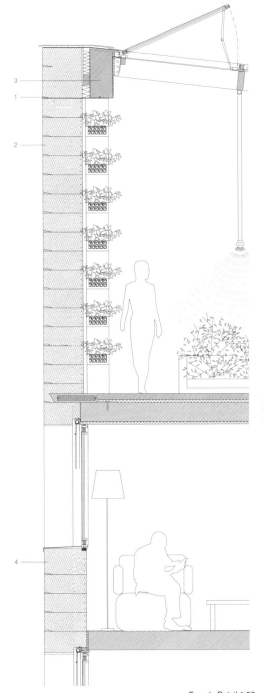

1. Vapor Retarder
2. 520 mm Precast Rammed Earth Unit
3. 140 mm Glulam Timber Beam
4. 380 mm Precast Rammed Earth Unit
   + Polypropylene Geogrid

Façade Detail 1:50

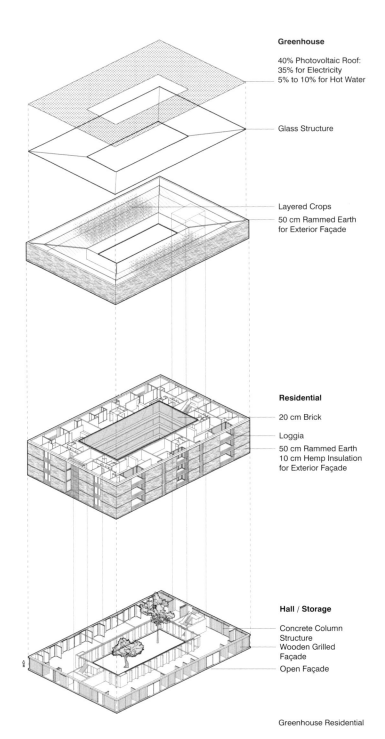

**Greenhouse**

40% Photovoltaic Roof:
35% for Electricity
5% to 10% for Hot Water

Glass Structure

Layered Crops
50 cm Rammed Earth
for Exterior Façade

**Residential**

20 cm Brick

Loggia
50 cm Rammed Earth
10 cm Hemp Insulation
for Exterior Façade

**Hall / Storage**

Concrete Column
Structure
Wooden Grilled
Façade

Open Façade

Greenhouse Residential

AGRICULTURAL LAND/RAMMED EARTH RESIDENCE

# WHITE LANDSCAPE

Heerlen is a city in the east of the Netherlands, near the border with Germany and Belgium. The area's main economic activity centered for many years on coal excavation, but now the main industry is harvesting of high-quality white sand. The Sibelco Company occupied a big part of the site and has many projects for development of this industrial activity. At the same time, some quarries have been abandoned, and need to be requalified into three landscaped projects.

The first part of this study was developed around two aspects: the organization of the territory and the constitution of the soil. These two concepts provide rich information about the situation at different scales within the Sibelco Quarry.

This huge and expansive terrain, which includes other extraction companies, must be considered at the scale of the city of Heerlen, and also at the scale of the Limburg

regional territory in the Netherlands. Historical maps are enlightening as to the history of extraction on site.

The second concept, soil, is a central question that can be answered by looking at geological formations. Much of the history of Heerlen comes from its soil and from the extraction of its resources, such as peat, coal and sand, which have shaped the landscape in this hilly region of Limburg, where the highest point in the Netherlands culminates at 322.50 meters.

Urbanization, development of agriculture, and transport networks are very strongly connected to the constitution of the ground and the soil. With this thought in mind, the west part of the Sibelco Quarry has to be considered on a different scale and will need to anticipate the future transformation of all local quarries over the next 20 years.

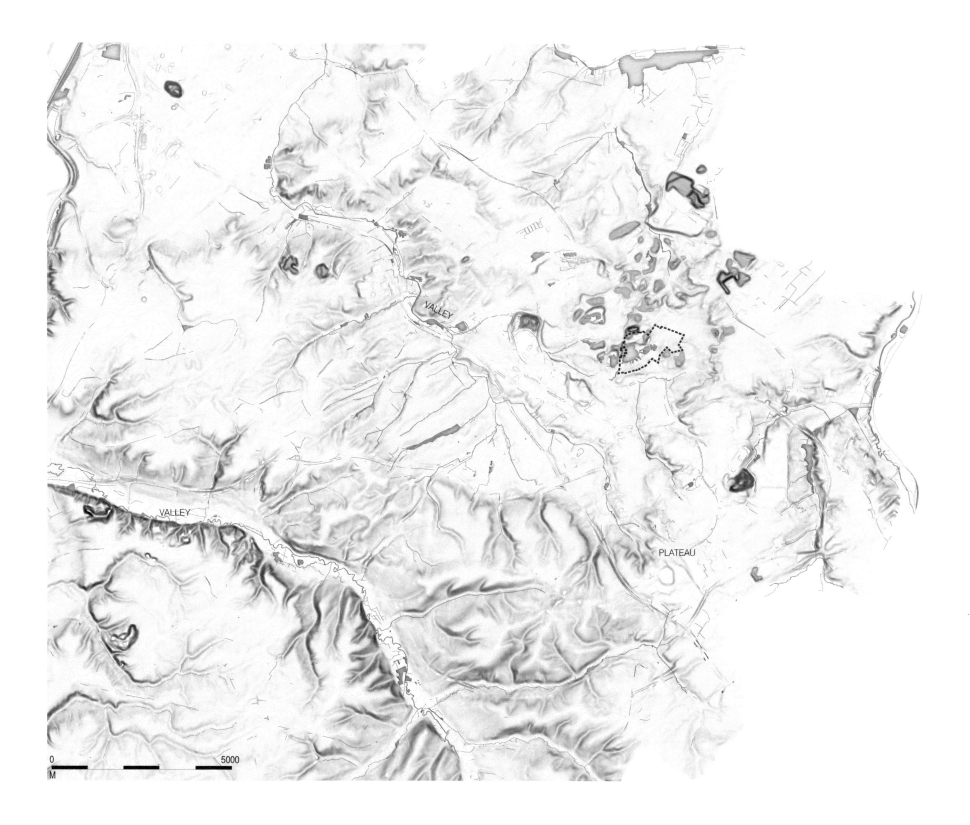

VALLEY

VALLEY

PLATEAU

0                                  5000
M

SAND    WATER    TRAIL

At the end of the coal mining period, the city implemented a large "black-to-green" plan. In this context the heaps were leveled and exploited as a deposit of embankments for earthworks. These lands were then abundantly planted. Within this environmental achievement, the old mining galleries were used as a source of geothermal energy.

The soil, both in present and ancient history, has never ceased to be a resource. From black to green, the old mining sites now serve as production sites, and can give new information as to the quality of the environment. For this reason, it is only natural that we wish to develop, within the framework of this project, the ecological and environmental virtues of the old sand pits.

We believe that the DNA of the quarries are organized around three elements: water, white sands and trails. Our proposal is to inaugurate the transformation of this territory, through the redevelopment of the narration from one of "exploitation" of the quarry into the aesthetic quality of the white sand and the reflection of the wellsprings of water.

We propose an ecologically ambitious project that develops biodiversity. The purposefulness of Miocene sand reveals the ancient history of the soil, its thickness and its complexity. Influenced by this archeological and geological data, we wish to create an exceptional landscape, and to be a witness to its richness as well as to the intricacies of its archives. We want to explore the density of its time, from the moment when it was a garden, to the historical stratification of the soil.

This exploration is not to be considered as a scientific reconstruction, but as an inspirational force from which to draw and to reveal the beauty of the site.

## DEVELOPMENT

As we have understood from the territorial study in the first phase, the global and gradual transformation of this operating territory will ultimately constitute a very large area, which refers directly to the area of Heerlen and to the whole territory of the Limburg Region.

From this perspective, it is necessary to imagine a global strategy that integrates several levels of landscape organization: trips and routes; diverse expressions of landscape; future activities and uses; developed biodiversity and coherence of profitable operating modes, adapted to the project desired for the future of this site.

It is necessary to reflect, with all the actors, on a new way of manufacturing, transforming and identifying this territory. This would be part of an ambitious model in terms of sustainable development, creating an ecosystem based on an idea of drawing from the source and constituting a narrative anchored in the very history of the site. From the DNA of the quarries, we have done experimental proposals and research with the basic elements of this "primitive and industrial" situation.

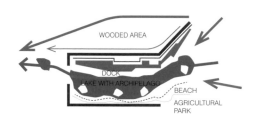

Strategy Archipelago

Landscape Connection: Water, Forest, Urbanization

Aerial View of the Lakes of Potsdam

Potsdam, Havel River

ParkstadTrail
Road
Urbanization
Forest
Agriculture
Sand
Water

0        500        1000

## LONG-TERM PROJECT

Connecting all of the quarries will be a long-term project, creating a great lake with facilities for the Heerlen population and the Limburg Region (like the example of Greater Berlin).

To discover a site, it is necessary to travel within it. The goal of this project is to constitute very gradually a set of paths that would circumscribe the whole network of lakes, according to modes of rearrangement that would link both pedestrians and cyclists as well as allowing cars to come near these future grounds for leisurely picnics, nature walks, and bird-watching.

This strategy will be developed gradually, while maintaining industrial activity. For this purpose, provisional and final arrangements can be devised to establish new relationships between the different parts of the site with a series of circular courses around the lakes, incorporating (temporary) floating walkways across the water to connect certain more definitive courses on land.

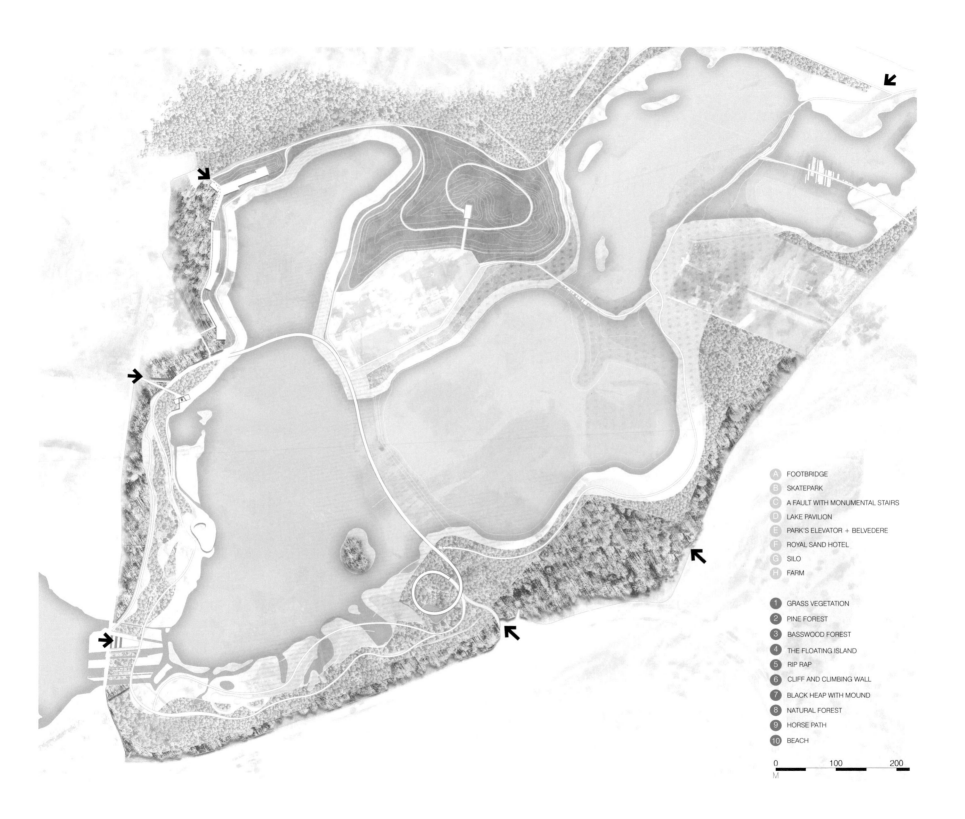

A FOOTBRIDGE
B SKATEPARK
C A FAULT WITH MONUMENTAL STAIRS
D LAKE PAVILION
E PARK'S ELEVATOR + BELVEDERE
F ROYAL SAND HOTEL
G SILO
H FARM

1 GRASS VEGETATION
2 PINE FOREST
3 BASSWOOD FOREST
4 THE FLOATING ISLAND
5 RIP RAP
6 CLIFF AND CLIMBING WALL
7 BLACK HEAP WITH MOUND
8 NATURAL FOREST
9 HORSE PATH
10 BEACH

0       100       200
M

BETULA    QUERCUS    MIXED FOREST DOMINATED BY TILIA    QUERCUS    BETULA + CORYLUS    PINE    HERBACEOUS LAYER    SHORE AND WATER

STRATIFICATION OF VEGETATION

ENTRANCE PAVILION

FOOTBRIDGE

LAKE PAVILION

# VERSAILLES

Versailles is a historic place for France, not only from a political point of view, but also from a global perspective for spatial planning and landscape organization. In Versailles – in particular thanks to the invention of André Le Notre, landscape designer to King Louis XIV – the site is reformulated with a new consideration for the grounds so as to rewrite the shape of the horizon, echoing infinity.

The Satory plateau is located south of the city of Versailles, isolated by its topography but also due to an army occupation, present on site for the last five centuries. The army having recently left the site, the opportunity arises to create the 8th district of Versailles.

Surrounded to the north by woodlands bordering the castle park, and to the south by forest land and the Bièvre ponds, Satory presents itself as a metropolitan island to the west of Paris.

The western part of this territory is the subject of this transformation project. It is occupied by test tracks for military equipment and was also used as a maneuver field. The urbanization of this new district is also linked to a metro line, planned as part of Greater Paris, which will open up this site, making it accessible in 15 to 20 minutes from the Saclay plateau, which is becoming the largest university site in France.

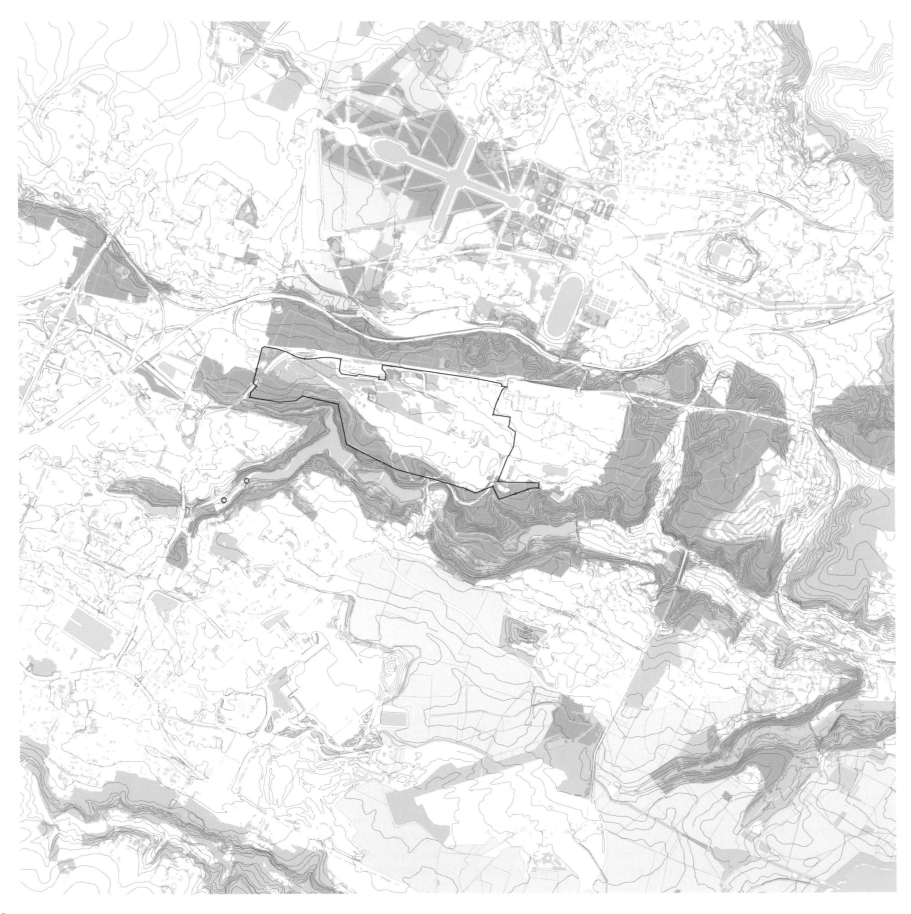

The project is organized around two founding concepts:
- an east to west geographical structure, which runs parallel to the park designed by André Le Notre
- creating a geometric north to south axis that connects two areas of wooded hills surrounding the site

The east-west orientation, which is the foundation of this project, reveals the depth of this landscape, opening the horizon towards the west. These views are the same as those that can be found along the main axis of the Grand Canal in the Parc du Château.

In the long term, it makes it possible to link the east and west part of the overall site more closely; it also articulates the sequence of different spaces and roads combining extremely different programs.

A long linear park bordering new housing ensembles is visually extended with technical and military equipment test tracks, the DNA of industrial research activity on this site.

A major landscaped axis to the north gives access to the entire site.

The north-south axis establishes the district's secondary distribution hierarchy, with three planted avenues, 30 and 60 meters wide. This generously dimensioned axis (similar to the main axis of the trident of the city of Versailles) has three goals:
- integrating a major traffic route connecting the north and south of the territory
- giving an identity to the entrance to this new district, echoing the main Versailles axis and organizing the historic center of the city
- visually linking the two forest and hilly landscapes to the north and south, ultimately the founding act of this 8th district of Versailles

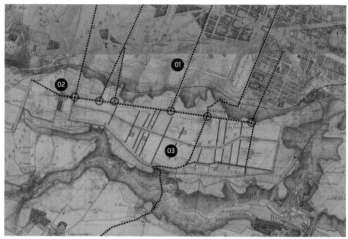

Versailles Geometry: North-South

Geographic Connection: East-West

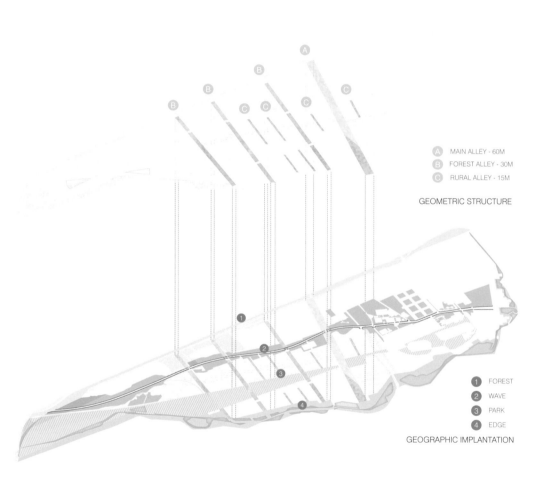

A  MAIN ALLEY - 60M
B  FOREST ALLEY - 30M
C  RURAL ALLEY - 15M

GEOMETRIC STRUCTURE

1  FOREST
2  WAVE
3  PARK
4  EDGE

GEOGRAPHIC IMPLANTATION

MAIN URBAN AXIS

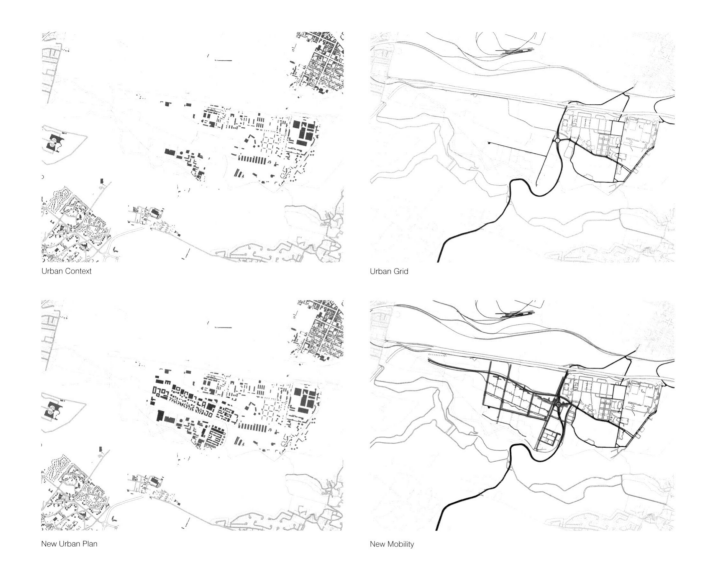

Urban Context

Urban Grid

New Urban Plan

New Mobility

## PUBLIC SPACE

The public spaces developed in this future district are characterized by major structuring factors as described above, but also through differentiated urban uses.

A major element in organizing the space is linked to the desire to create a territory for pedestrians and cyclists, and to group together all of the private parking in silo parking lots, which may be transformed later on.

Large pedestrian islands with adapted pathways offer a certain residential comfort, where landscaped spaces are practiced according to a more Anglo- Saxon model.

More specific public spaces such as the central park, the future square of the new Versailles-Satory metro station and nearby squares for residents, are thus offered in addition to the main landscaped axis.

The general hydrology of the site will be organized using landscape bioswales on the surface, which resonate with the invention of the Versailles landscapes, where water was a major element throughout the gardens and parks in the 17th century.

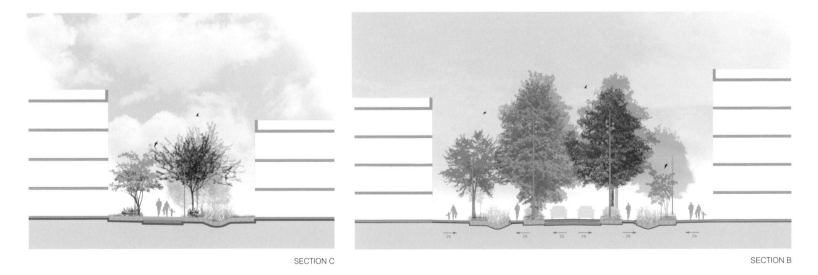

SECTION A

SECTION C

SECTION B

## BORDER DISTRICT

The first micro-district to be developed is located at the edge of the southern side of the Bièvre pond forest. It includes a program of 700 housing units, a school, a multi-story car park and an office building.

The housing program will develop several typologies; collective, stacked townhouses, and grouped individual dwellings.

It is organized starting with a square form, in the footsteps of old existing paths. The heart of this district develops a large majority of housing, with pedestrian alleys.

A meadow in the center decorated with a few trees offers a small park for the inhabitants. The school is positioned between this meadow and the major, 60-meter-wide planted avenue that constitutes the main axis. Parking is grouped together in a silo parking lot to the north, and one-way streets will offer very little longitudinal parking. The height of the buildings in this district will not exceed five levels.

TYPE 1: Intermediate Housing

TYPE 2: Grouped Individual Houses

TYPE 3: Overlayed Apartments

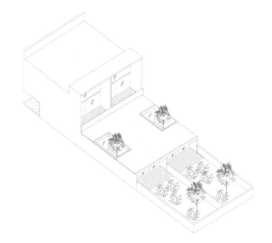

TYPE 4: Attached Individual Houses

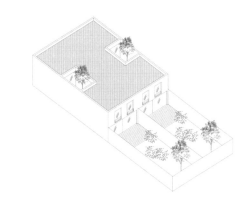

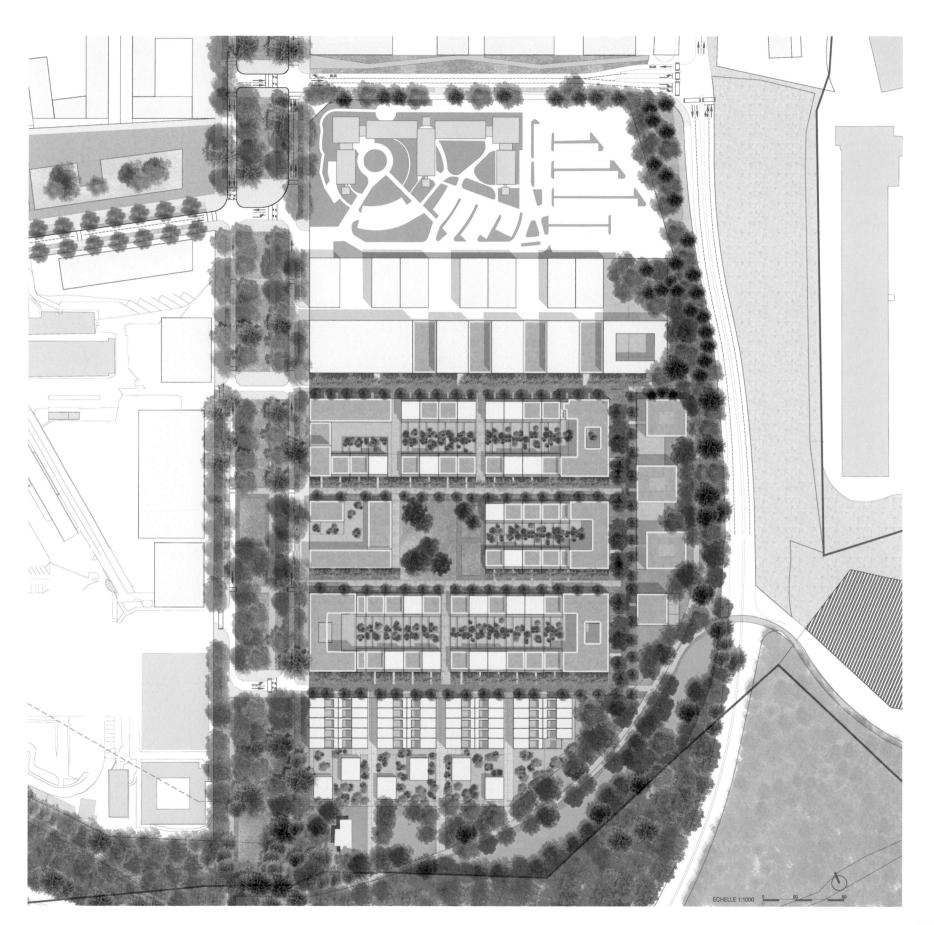

ECHELLE 1:1000

247

## HABITAT

The question of housing quality is fundamental to sustaining such a district. The variety of living arrangements must respond to new social constellations and relationships within families, which have changed dramatically in recent years.

For this reason, it seems important to offer different types of accommodation, with exterior extensions: gardens, terraces, patios, etc. For this reason and in this context, associating collective housing building with stacked housing units is particularly interesting, as well as housing that offers apartments on one level or the option of duplexes. For this "intermediate band" housing, the question of thresholds is essential.

Making sure that each entry point is individualized, superimposing housing units or dealing with overlooking apartments are all subjects to be treated with care, to bring forward new ways of living together. The study carried out on the first project pays particular attention to intimacy within the housing units and to "extension spaces".

New goals are suggested by the community in terms of sustainable development.

This translates here into using durable materials: brick and wood, and to designing relatively compact buildings, which reduces energy consumption. The orientation of the buildings, through the use of wide windows, which open onto the landscape adds to the quality and comfort of the homes.

All of these objectives have been studied for this first model project, which helps to determine the overall orientation of future housing projects in this new district.

# THE DEPTH OF LANDSCAPE

Saint-Jacques-de-la-Lande Lecture*

## Jean-Pierre Pranlas-Descours

*In the early 90s, the city council of Saint-Jacques-de-la-Lande in the periphery of Rennes (Brittany) decided to reorganize its territory mainly by creating a new city center. From the beginning, this ambitious project has become a reaction to a general tendency: the dilution of the territory in sprawlings cities.*

*Before talking about the creation and development of the project, I would like to mention several ideas which are necessary to understand the transformation of metropolitan territories as well as their densities.*

*This lecture was presented in April 2005 at Columbia University (NY) and at Cornell University (NY).

Image on the previous page: Saint-Jacques-de-la-Lande Cemetery Pavilion

Jean-Pierre Pranlas-Descours

## Metropolitan Territories

The foundations of our occidental urban culture have changed considerably throughout the 20th century. Unlike before, periods of marked urbanization are no longer defined and city limits are no longer factors of social organization and regulation. This slow transition in occidental history marks a decline of urban continuity figures in our culture.

Within this context, the process of separation and distancing modifies the basic relationship between social bodies and public space. With contemporary urban spaces becoming more and more expansive, their fragmented nature is exacerbated by autonomous architectural objects that reject the premise of territorial homogeneity. Existing links between local and global concepts demand reconsideration. It therefore now seems that no single unitary urban concept would be capable of giving direction for the extension of contemporary cities. If there is an identity crisis in the urban world, it can be found within our insertion models, which, as we have seen, are intimately linked to defined and recognizable urban figures. These figures, in particular those used for organizing public space, generate social ties in contemporary cities and provide a spatial environment for their growth.

The contemporary city, which has emerged all over the world, is of another type and has not yet invented new systems of stable regulation as seen throughout history. These cities are no longer contained within their own, self-imposed limits. They tend to spread over larger territories, composing a disturbing number of "heterotopias" that group together abandoned urban spaces and developable lands.

A new kind of space has appeared in the contemporary city: parking lots, post-industrial zones, train stations, airports, etc. Today, we no longer live in cities but in metropolitan territories whose limits we can hardly define, demonstrating once again the crisis of confronting traditional models and new occidental cities. André Corboz evoked the figure of the palimpsest. New positions and new places that create hitherto unknown urban situations are emerging within larger territories and the question of scale is no longer valid; this phenomenon concerns an average-sized city as much as a megalopolis. It is not a question of dimension but of events.

The 20th century thus saw the development of a type of urban growth that had no relation with the slow and painstaking forma urbis. Connection systems and development networks now link spaces, once foreign to one another, in new geographies that are very artificial, and the city of today grows as a succession of enclaves, an accumulation of cultural minorities that constitute juxtaposed "oceans of solitude" within each territory.

## Landscape: Condition of a Project

There are some very specific conditions to an urban project that provide it with a foundation and an orientation. In the early 90s, the territory of St-Jacques-de-la-Lande had all the characteristics of a suburb that had been ruined by years of wild urban planning. During this time, important infrastructures had been built and had divided the town, creating segregations within the area. The ring road of Rennes runs north of Saint Jacques, separating its first district from the rest of its territory and, in the south, the airport of Rennes isolates the second district, the historical center, from the rest of the town.

From west to east, there are other separations: the bullet train line between Rennes and southern Brittany as well as the 177 secondary road run in the same direction, from west to east. Among many remarkable elements, there are military camps which are not under the city council's control; these are formed like small islands in the middle of the territory. Because of its almost desperate urban situation, the planning project was nearly cancelled. Nevertheless, in spite of these factors, and because the mayor believed that only a high voltage line could bring more damage to the landscape, he decided to undertake this ambitious project and to organize a competition for the new city center with several architects.

The feeling of nothingness came from the sight of a very delicate and complex landscape. Analyzing and understanding the landscape allowed a series of dramatic changes to be undertaken. A remarkable feature of the landscape was the woodlands and bushes, cutting and creating a series of close and distant skylines. These folds in the landscape would create great thickness on the ground; some skylines were close and others were far away. This perception was enhanced by slight topographical differences and a constant movement of the ground that defined a plateau where farms formely existed. This series of greenery and bushes was an invitation to go further into the landscape in order to discover new perspectives.

Closer analysis showed that many of the real estate plots were of similar size: approximately 120 by 120 meters. Paradoxically, this dimension is close to the Cerda plan in Barcelona; Breton cows were in fact grazing in a perfect urban system. Several geometrical and geographical themes emerge in this urban project and skylines, ground and geometry are used as tools to draw and define hierarchies within the landscape. Units related to this landscape can be defined as follows:
- a farm and a manor on a plateau
- hillsides towards the west over the wide landscape
- easily flooded, non-constructible meadows
- on the east part are new houses adapting to the contour lines

Jean-Pierre Pranlas-Descours

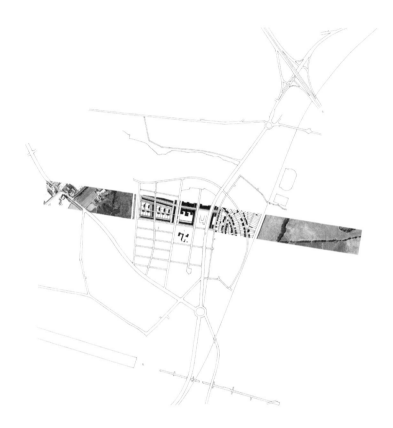

## Territory

The city of St-Jacques-de-la-Lande is a split territory. Since it is very close to the city of Rennes (10-minute drive to the station and 15 minutes to the center), it needed to be reset. However, the only physical link is road 177 connecting three neighborhoods within the city and, at the time, the regional administration wanted to reorganize this infrastructure. A highway with no real relation to the new city center and its redevelopment project was to be built. As we have seen in other metropolitan areas, one of the main characteristics of these types of roads that go from the cities to the suburbs, is new urban landscapes organized around billboards and low-quality buildings.

We wanted to avoid the Potemkin phenomenon as referred to in Adolf Loos' "Trotzdem"[1] in which he criticized the 'Ring' in Vienna. He mentions Potemkin, advisor to Catherine II, empress of Russia, who invited the tsarina to the Russian steppes and, in order to show her the great work that he was undertaking for the development of Russia, showed huge paintings representing hypothetical cities put on top of the hills.

This urban semblance prior to our modernity seemed to be premonitory. In Saint Jacques, building a highway at the same time as a new neighborhood gave us the opportunity to think about the urban depth and the density of the space around this road. Thus, our concept developed into that of a road crossing this territory. The 2 km north-south road would be intersected by its equivalent going from east to west through this territory. Along this line, we recommended high-density shapes and forms. In an asymmetrical context created from the existing organization of the site, a sparsely populated area (including existing historical houses) and large natural areas would create balance with new areas along one transversal line. This road was to be the first structural element of the project and the guideline for decision making throughout its duration.

Several development areas related to geography were to be defined:
- a high-density sector with housing programs and public equipment with a mixed-use concept east of the city
- a residential area, with both apartment buildings and individual houses, to the west
- shops and office buildings along the boulevard. In order to settle the city into the site, we wanted to create building programs related to geography and to their place in the territory
- a series of urban pieces emerging from an orthogonal scheme: little open islands with a coherent development of building programs related to general rules of the neighborhood
- public spaces with dimensions that could be determined from the main road

1 Loos, Adolf: "Trotzdem." Innsbruck, 1931.

Master Plan 1994

## Building a City

Creating a new housing district is always very complex. There are no classical terms defining the architecture in St-Jacques-de-la-Lande and if there were, it would imply artificial formalism. Analyzing and observing the territory led to a certain number of building principles related to the site. Some principles came around while building the first apartment building where we carefully followed the natural shape of the ground. A real ground project as well as a built topography were created on the whole site and concrete bases emerging from the ground would provide a base for all new buildings, whatever their architecture. Thus, the project becomes a stratification of various layers, especially in the central area where we planned a mixed project (housing, services, shopping center, etc.). The first building had shops on the ground floor with apartments on the second to fourth floors and penthouses on the two upper levels.

The transition between landscape stratification and typological superposition was used as an example for the urban project. The shopping center was the first important program the city council wished to build. This first project was originally supposed to be a typical suburban project: a shopping center along a road. However, we wanted this traditional project to become more adapted to urban life, and not just create a "box" alongside a highway with parking lots surrounding the box. Instead, we considered each element of the shopping center and we tried to integrate them into the urban project, associating this shopping center with public buildings and housing programs. Thus, 5,000 m² of the shopping center program was directly injecting into several housing programs, other shops, and a library. Since it was the first important program, it was built in a landscape between the city and the countryside; it was a foundation of the global urban project, a basis for future urbanization.

We built a kind of plateau from the highest part of the site on the north with 30,000 m² surface area overall. The shopping center was then built as a big grocery store with apartments in the floors above. There were two basic ideas for this building's architecture: strong load-bearing materials and great care for the façade. Since the city council wanted 'real' architecture for this project, it overlooked construction and only afterwards was the building sold to the company running the shopping center.

Once the base had been built, we built apartments above, with direct access from the street. Galleries leading from the apartments to the elevators and the staircases in order gave direct vertical access to the shopping center. This way of entering the building has become very popular and most people living in the apartments now have their own shopping cart.

Jean-Pierre Pranlas-Descours

Then, the big question was the top of the shopping center. It became a terrace for the apartments and we designed a plum tree orchard as if it were a natural continuation of the private gardens and terraces of the apartments. A basin watering the terrace is dividing it, as in Moorish palaces.

The other main question for a shopping center was the parking area; parking lots are continually becoming important elements within our visual landscape. Our first suggestion was to build one-third of the parking spaces underneath the shopping center. However, the second idea was to use exterior parking lots as a link between the city and the countryside. Thus, on the north part of the site, the parking area was designed as a landscape with one-third parking and two-thirds planted spaces with an old farm building kept onsite.

This space between is important as an urban link within city suburbs, for example the farm building later became a building for associations. I find it very important to rethink these neglected sites in contemporary cities, themselves part of metropolitan territories. They must not be embellished but they must be part of the conversation for constituting cities in order to change our mind about dividing public sites.

## The Library

The last important part of the project was the library. This building fills the southwest corner of the project and is also a link between the shopping center and the main square in front of the city hall.

It was, at first, difficult to build a public building in a quite homogeneous housing area and we had to think it through because most cities accumulate autonomous architectural buildings. However, one must ask how autonomous a public building can really be within a city?

We had various concerns:
- the built building at an urban scale
- the tectonic principles of urban buildings
- the extension of public space from the building

According to these three points, we developed this building in terms of its autonomy. Considering the heights of the attached buildings and the design of the surrounding façades, we decided to divide the building into three layers:
- a base of concrete pillars
- a central element made of precast sections
- a zinc plate covering

Once we had determined the main principle we wanted to create a series of open plan surfaces inside the building (15 × 30 m). The structure of these open surfaces was extended towards the outside by adding precast elements, allowing an abstract concrete lattice to disrupt the scale of the surrounding buildings. Through this technique, we wanted to showcase public space within the city on a monumental scale. With this process, we sought continuity of public space inside the building by creating a central courtyard where, thanks to precise lighting work, the whole library can be seen.

Structurally, the building is conceived as a sort of large meccano-type construction, with apparent precast load-bearing components connected by poured-on-site concrete elements. The precast parametric columns and beams are constituted of a single lower layer of white concrete, as is the floor structure, that also acts as form for the poured-on-site upper slab. We then added 8 cm of flooring and beams to 7 cm of precast concrete flooring. Suspending wooden floors are added to this inverted system so as to give a certain unity with regards to the materials, for the interior and the exterior. Once the open plan surfaces had been built, we designed all of the furniture for the library, creating comfortable and intimate spaces. Inside the library, glass walls allow users to be a part of the city while maintaining high levels of intimacy.

Jean-Pierre Pranlas-Descours

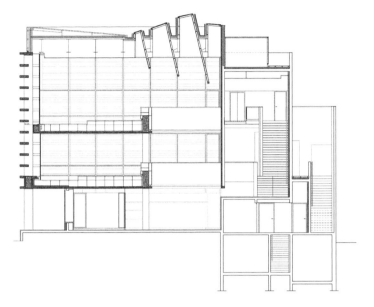

## The Project as Process

These personal architectural projects in the general urban project made me think about several principles for the edification of projects to come. I did not want to establish rules about architectural aesthetics or a modern pre-language architecture (as Baron Haussmann would have done); nevertheless, I wanted to think about the composition of this project and others to come.

Themes relating to the ground, to the relationship between landscape and its horizontal lines, and to topological associations were the real questions in this project. Despite the fact that today there is a habit of mixing architectural objects, we wanted each project to make the most of this process that is building a city, taking into consideration constraints that come with building private or public buildings.

The 1994 plan, which, at first glance, seems classic, was only the first layer of the project to come. The difference between this plan and that of March 2005 shows the profound evolution of the project.

According to common principles, each urban project has its own urban coherence depending on its programs, general location, and the ability of architects to adapt within a global project. Although the scale is very different, it is possible to compare this context with the constitution of New York blocks, as is mentioned by Rem Koolhas in Delirious New York. Each project balances very different volumes, but each with the same density. In Saint Jacques, for example, a 200-apartment program is developed in the denser part of the city, in continuity with the shopping center with necessary schools for the neighborhood; an illustration of this very process.

For this project, the architect built all the public facilities on the concrete ground floor of the building, with apartments above. We had a hard time adapting to the natural ground and creating pathways for the local children. The problem was to have all these blocks next to one another and to find links unrelated to pre-established aesthetic rules. The links between the blocks are porches, continuous views on both sides of the streets, the concrete beds for the buildings and horizontal levels from one building to another. This process was also developed in the western part of the city with different kinds of housing: apartment buildings, attached houses and individual houses.

Within this urban project, every new project was always developed in relation to the same density for each block. Over time, a growing number of attached houses were built instead of individual houses and the community outreach in those areas was much stronger. For the last built project, the main issue was having the steepest slope on site.

This tense relationship with the ground, the key to the project, progressively organized orientation and contour lines to the west. The idea of the project became more and more related to mixed housing and its relation to topography. Among other architects already working in the denser, eastern side of the city, the Dutch team Claus and Kaan from Rotterdam suggested building a tower using existing horizontal lines to create a new line. This would now be possible as the discussion is always based on what exists and what is yet to come.

This tower was to be a demonstration of this difference where it is possible to change the rule in an existing urban culture. The urban rules are like a rocket heading for planet Mars: as it progresses in the atmosphere, it loses various levels to send the satellite to its destination. At the end, after the satellite has done its job, it disintegrates. In Saint-Jacques-de-la-Lande, the city is created from projects and not from rules that freeze any urban and architectural evolution. Here, the city council took responsibility and stuck to it, which made the process possible.

## The Matter of Cities and Public Space

The city has to be built.
It can only be built with long-lasting materials.
The construction must stick to existing materials.
Saint-Jacques-de-la-Lande has 8,500 inhabitants and since it is not a particularly wealthy town, it must be built with modest means, but with good quality building (the library, for example) as was decided by the city council. Quality materials were used on the site: raw concrete, wood and no PVC windows, for instance. Then each architect building on site used these various materials for their personal architecture.

The process was the same for public spaces; using simple and inexpensive materials for a precise drawing of public space. Social and financial investment was very important for the city. Therefore, in collaboration with the amazing landscape architect team Bruel-Delmar, we sought coherence within a great variety of public spaces; for the parking lot of the shopping center as well as for the private gardens. In order to structure public space, we used water flow systems for water collection in basins (Brittany is a very rainy area). These basins then defined the limits of certain public spaces and there was no use for a complex and sophisticated public design, a factor which is not always the case in most urban projects nowadays.

Jean-Pierre Pranlas-Descours

Public space is an open place defined by users' habits; architects cannot always anticipate them and the community must express itself. There is an evolution in the use of public space in Saint-Jacques-de-la-Lande and we now wonder about the relationship between the areas for cars and those for pedestrians. We are thinking of leaving the north-south road for pedestrians only.

Along this road are most shops and public facilities as well as a great variety of public spaces:
- parking spaces for the shopping center
- a main commercial high street
- a square in front of city hall
- parks and gardens for city hall and the manor
- high school and gymnasium
- cemetery

We wanted our project in Saint-Jacques-de-la-Lande to be intimately related to the landscape and the ground is the basic element in this strategy. We developed site urbanism leading to a strategical urbanism. Research on contemporary housing is essential in this process. We did not want to refer to a morphological model; we wanted to create this new area according to this process of composition, allowing us to show that all levels of architecture are involved in the creation of contemporary territories.

We used the depth of landscape to imagine the project, but we tried to create a philosophy to design the infrastructure as well as the details of the library.

"The city is an architecture", Aldo Rossi said 40 years ago.
Today "the territory is now an architecture".

## EPILOGUE

*At the end of a long period of 20 years (1992–2012), a new project to build a church (2009–2018) began on the initiative of the Archbishop of Rennes, Monsignor d'Ornellas.*

*After many meetings, the choice of architect fell very naturally on Alvaro Siza. His experience with this type of building had already been demonstrated by the very beautiful Church of Santa Maria de Marco de Canaveses, north of Porto, and other chapel projects.*

*The design was the subject of many discussions between the Archbishop and Alvaro Siza, particularly for the interior organization of this church, which developed on the first floor of the building.*

*Located in the heart of this development, close to a manor house and its chapel, this building has created an extraordinary anchoring point for the community of new inhabitants, whatever their beliefs, and thus brought about a new identity for this district.*

*Our office collaborated on the outside of this building, which is a unitary volume in white concrete with very few openings, like a Cistercian church. Inside, in the upper chapel, the space is bathed in natural light, the origin of which cannot be perceived, thanks to a generous spatiality referring to an extraordinary spiritual dimension.*

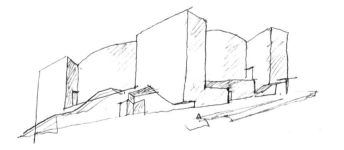

Jean-Pierre Pranlas-Descours

# AUTHORS

**Kenneth Frampton**

KENNETH FRAMPTON is an architect, architecture critic, historian, and professor of architecture at the Graduate School of Architecture and Planning at Columbia University, New York. He is known for his writings on twentieth-century architecture. His works include *Modern Architecture: A Critical History* (1980) and *Studies in Tectonic Culture* (1997). Kenneth Frampton captured a wide audience with his architectural teaching based on his essay *Towards a Critical Regionalism* (1983). In 2002, a collection of his writing spanning a period of 35 years was published under the title *Labour, Work and Architecture*. He has published *Five North American Architects: An Anthology by Kenneth Frampton* (2012), *Genealogy of Modern Architecture: A Comparative Critical Analysis of Built Form* (2014), *L'altro Movimento Moderno,* edited by Ludovica Molo (2015). He was appointed Commander of the Order of the British Empire (CBE) in 2021. He received the Golden Lion for Lifetime Achievement at the Venice Biennale of Architecture in 2021, and the Thomas Jefferson Foundation Medal in Architecture in 2022.

**Ashley Simone**

ASHLEY SIMONE is an editor, writer, and curator whose practice operates at the intersection of art, architecture, and culture. Her writing has appeared in numerous books and journals published by Actar, BOMB Magazine, Lars Müller Publishers, Oro Editions, and Thames and Hudson. Among other volumes on architecture and urbanism, she is the editor of *A Genealogy of Modern Architecture* (2015) and *The Other Modern Movement* (2021) by Kenneth Frampton, *Absurd Thinking Between Art and Design* by Allan Wexler (2017), *Two Journeys* by Michael Webb (2018), *Frank Gehry Catalogue Raisonné, Volume One, 1954–1978* by Jean-Louis Cohen (2020), *Occupation: Boundary, Art, Architecture, and Culture at the Water* by Cathy Simon (2021), and she is a co-editor of *In Search of African American Space* (2020). She is an Associate Professor at Pratt Institute School of Architecture.

**Jean-Pierre Pranlas-Descours**

JEAN-PIERRE PRANLAS-DESCOURS qualified as an architect at the École d'Architecture de Versailles and received a Masters in Medieval History from the École des Hautes Études en Sciences Sociales. He won the French Academy in Rome competition at the Villa Medicis in 1986. His architectural and urban projects cross the different scales for a sustainable world. He won several urban competitions in Europe (Barcelona, Reykjavik, El Prat de Llobregat) and has realized housing and public buildings in France. He has taught in different architecture faculties, at the École Nationale des Ponts et Chaussées and is presently full professor at the Ecole Nationale d'Architecture de Paris-Malaquais and has been visiting professor at the City College in New York. He received the Robert Auzelle prize for the Urban project for the Bottiere-Chenaie/Nantes. He was awarded several architectural prizes, as the International S-ARCH for the World Best Public Building 2020, and the D'A architectural review 2020 for the Chambre des Métiers et de l'Artisanat in Lille, and the Holcim Foundation Gold Award Asia-Pacific for the Yuzhong project in 2021. He received the Honour Medaille of the Académie Architecture (Paris) in 2012, where he became an official member in 2022.

TEAM

**Orso Angeli**, Valentina Acierno, Nathalie Apostolatos, Valérie Baglione, Luisa Barbudo, **Colette Brice**, Benjamin Bancel, Jeremie Bedel, Véronique Bonnard, Émilie Bonnet, Stéphanie Bru, Delphine Bresson, Émilie Bohec, Jessica Norberg Berspang, Louise de Chatellus, Cyril Chenebeau, Agnieszka Cipariani, Agnès Cremel, Antoine Crupi, Gustav Ducloz, Yoann Dupouy, Vanessa Fernandez, Akiko Koba, Marylène Gallon, **Antoine Guilhem Ducléon**, Marianne Seyhan, Marion Dufet, Marianne Seyhan, Cyrille Fremiot, Arnaud Freycenon, Charles Gallet, Sabine Germond, **Julie Heathcote-Smith**, Flore Teyssendier de la Serve, Michael Kaplan, **Pauline Lacroix-Ducousseau**, Christophe Lachassagne, Hélène Le Madec, **Maxime Léger**, **Pauline Lamperier**, Flora La Sita, Eunju Lee, Laetitia Lesage, Brieuc Le Coz, Alice Luraghi, Christel Macchiaro, Odile Michaud, Mireille Mussino, Samira Nagy, Magdalena Pawlak, Enrique Penichet, Fabien Pinault, Charlotte Poux-Fourtane, Chiara Porcu, Anne Roullet, Sémélé Sangla, Paolo Tarabusi, Stéphanie Touffet, Maia Tüür, Chloé Traband, Lena Weiss, **Zhaoying Zhu**

## INDEX OF PROJECTS

### MOUNTAIN HOUSING

Dates: 2012–2016

Location: Seyssins, France

Client: Peaks Immobilier

Architects: PDAA

Lanscape: Catherine Mosbach

Total floor area: 790 m²

Team: Louise de Chatellus, Marion Lapierre-Auber, Delphine Bresson

Engineers: MATTE

Models: Marion Dufet

Photographs: Antoine Guilhem-Ducléon

### ICELAND TOURIST PAVILION

Dates: 2020 Competition

Location: Mytavn, Island

Client: Landowner of the farm

Architects: PDAA

Total floor area: 355 m²

Team: Zhaoying Zhu, Maxime Léger

### PAVE BLANC HOUSINGS PHASE 1

Dates: 2008–2013

Location: Clamart, France

Client: Immobilière 3F

Architects: PDAA

Landscape: Atelier Paysages Bruel Delmar

Total floor area: 3,790 m²

Team: Colette Brice, Louise de Chatellus, Matylène Gallon

Engineers: TALBOT, EVP, WOR, TERAO, Philippe Talbot & Associés

Models: Marianne Seyhan

Photographs: Antoine Guilhem-Ducléon

## CHAMBER OF TRADES AND CRAFTS

**Dates:** 2008–2019

**Location:** Lille, France

**Client:** Chamber of Trades and Crafts

**Architects:** PDAA, KAAN architecten

**Landscape:** TN+

**Total floor area:** 13,500 m²

**Team:** Christophe Banderier (KAAN), Sebastian van Damme (KAAN), Gustav Ducloz (PDAA), Paolo Faleschini (KAAN), Raluca Firicel (KAAN), Marylène Gallon (PDAA), Michael Geensen (KAAN), Renata Gilio (KAAN), Julie Heathcote-Smith (PDAA), Maud Minault (KAAN), Hannes Ochmann (KAAN), Vincent Panhuysen (KAAN), Fabien Pinault (KAAN), Ismael Planelles (KAAN), Ana Rivero Esteban (KAAN), Anne Roullet (PDAA), Dikkie Scipio (KAAN), Marianne Seyhan (PDAA)

**Engineers:** EVP, URBATEC, TESS, MARTIN & GUIHENEUF, Creacept restauration

**Models:** Marianne Seyhan

**Photographs:** FG+SG , Antoine Guilhem-Ducléon, Sebastian van Damme.

## TECHNICAL SCHOOL

**Dates:** 2007–2009

**Location:** Nantes, France

**Client:** Association Ouvrière des Compagnons du Devoir du Tour de France

**Architects:** PDAA

**Total floor area:** 1,796 m²

**Team:** Colette Brice, Jeremy Bedel

**Engineers:** EVP, BEThAC, Concept Ingénierie

**Models:** Marianne Seyhan

**Photographs:** Antoine Guilhem-Ducléon

## LIMA MODERN ART MUSEUM

**Dates:** 2016 Competition

**Location:** Lima, France

**Client:** MALI Museum

**Architects:** PDAA

**Total floor area:** 6,250 m²

**Team:** Gustav Ducloz, Christine Dalnoky

**Engineers:** EVP

**Models:** Marion Dufet

## PANTIN CORNER DWELLINGS

**Dates:** 2010–2013

**Location:** Pantin, France

**Client:** Kaufman & Broad

**Architects:** PDAA

**Total floor area:** 1,145 m²

**Team:** Gustav Ducloz, Yasmine Gazzi, Delphine Bresson, Matylène Gallon

**Engineers:** IC, TEC

**Models:** Marianne Seyhan

**Photographs:** Antoine Guilhem-Ducléon

## PAVE BLANC HOUSINGS PHASE 2

**Dates:** 2013–2015

**Location:** Clamart, France

**Client:** Immobilière 3F

**Architects:** PDAA

**Landscape:** Atelier Paysages Bruel Delmar

**Total floor area:** 2,000 m²

**Team:** Colette Brice, Louise de Chatellus, Marylène Gallon

**Engineers:** TALBOT, EVP, WOR, TERAO, Philippe Talbot & Associés

**Models:** Marianne Seyhan

**Photographs:** Antoine Guilhem-Ducléon

## NANTES DWELLINGS

**Dates:** 2011–2015

**Location:** Nantes, France

**Client:** Ouest Immo OTI

**Architects:** PDAA

**Landscape:** Atelier Paysages Bruel Delmar

**Total floor area:** 5,850 m²

**Team:** Louise de Chatellus, Anne Roullet

**Engineers:** INEX, EXECOME

**Models:** Marianne Seyhan

**Photographs:** Antoine Guilhem-Ducléon

## LILLE OFFICES

**Dates:** 2008–2014

**Location:** Lille, France

**Client:** Soreli

**Architects:** PDAA

**Total floor area:** 6,605 m²

**Team:** Louise de Chatellus

**Engineers:** EVP, INEX, SL2EC

**Models:** Marianne Seyhan

**Photographs:** Antoine Guilhem-Ducléon

## MIXED-USE OFFICES

**Dates:** 2015–2018

**Location:** Lille, France

**Client:** Ervefel

**Architects:** PDAA

**Total floor area:** 4,500 m²

**Team:** Louise de Chatellus, Marion Lapierre Auber, Julie Heathcote-Smith, Orso Angeli, Delphine Bresson, Luisa Barbudo

**Engineers:** EVP, PROJEX, SL2EC

**Models:** Marianne Seyhan

**Photographs:** Antoine Guilhem-Ducléon

## PESSAC MIXED-TYPOLOGY DWELLINGS

**Dates:** 2020–(in progress)

**Location:** Pessac, France

**Client:** Kaufman & Broad

**Architects:** PDAA, LNA

**Landscape:** PDAA

**Programs:** 124 housings and 1 hotel

**Team:** Julie Heathcote-Smith, Zhaoying Zhu, Pauline Lamperier, Maxime Léger

**Engineers:** MATH, MEB, VIVIEN

**Models:** Pauline Lacroix-Ducousseau

## YUZHONG URBAN AND LANDSCAPE DEVELOPMENT

**Dates:** 2019–(in progress)

**Location:** Yuzhong, China

**Client:** City of Yuzhong

**Architects:** PDAA

**Total site area:** 11,380,000 m²

**Team:** Caroline Bouteloup(CSTB), Cristina Garcez (CSTB), Jian Guan (CSTB), Abdel Lakel (CSTB), Maxime Léger (PDAA), Emilien Parron (CSTB), Zhaoying Zhu (PDAA)

**Engineers:** CSTB

**Photographs:** JP Pranlas-Descours

## HEERLEN QUARRIES TRANSFORMATION

**Dates:** 2016–2017

**Location:** Heerlen, Netherlands

**Client:** Sibelco Groeve

**Architects:** PDAA

**Landscape:** Atelier Christine Dalnoky

**Total site area:** 332,700 m²

**Team:** Yoann Dupouy, Daniel Pierlot, Akiko Koba, Chloé Traband

**Engineers:** SEPIA

**Photographs:** JP Pranlas-Descours

## VERSAILLES-SATORY URBAN DEVELOPMENT

**Dates:** 2015–(in progress)

**Location:** Satory, France

**Client:** Établissement public d'aménagement Paris-Saclay

**Architects:** PDAA

**Landscape:** Atelier Christine Dalnoky

**Total site area:** 2,360,000 m²

**Team:** Yoann Dupouy, Akiko Koba, Hélène Le Madec, Pauline Lamperier, Orso Angeli, Brieu Le Coz, Chloé Traband, Colette Brice

**Engineers:** EGIS, Atelier LD, SEPHIA

**Models:** ARTEFACT

## CREDITS

Rosalind Krauss. Diagram, Sculpture in the expanded field: page 11
© Rosalind Krauss

Mies van der Rohe Ludwig. Illinois Institute of Technology. Chicago, 1939–41. Master Plan, General Studies, Preliminary Studies. Campus. Aerial perspective. Preliminary version: page 13
DIGITAL IMAGE © 07/06/2022, The Museum of Modern Art/Scala, Florence

Mies van der Rohe Ludwig. Early Study for the Library and Administration Building, Illinois Institute of Technology, Chicago, Illinois, Perspective: page 13
© 2018 Artists Rights Society (ARS), New York / VG Bild-Kunst, Bonn

Quinta da Malagueira, Evora, Portugal: page 15
© Roberto Collova

Alvar Aalto. Master Plan of Imatra, Finland, 1946: page 202
Alvar Aalto. Scheme of main spatial axis with natural zones, Master Plan of Imatra, Finland, 1946: page 203
© Alvar Aalto Museum

Photo of Potsdam, Havel River: page 228
© PMSG/Steven Ritz

Sketch of Anastasis Church, Saint-Jacques de-la-Lande: page 262
© Alvaro Siza

Photo of Anastasis Church, Saint-Jacques de-la-Lande: page 263
© João Morgado

Photographs: Antoine Guilhem-Ducléon
except:
pages 58, 66, 72, 78, 81, 83, 85, 86, 87, 88, 89: Fernando Guerra (FG+SG)
pages 17, 65, 70, 71, 74, 76 left, 77 right, 91: Sebastian van Damme

## ACKNOWLEDGEMENTS

Jean-Pierre Pranlas-Descours would like to thank:
Kenneth Frampton for his support and friendship.
Ashley Simone for her accurate observation of my work.
All of the developers and partners who give me the opportunity to realize my architectural projects.
Alvaro Siza for the marvelous collaboration on the Anastasis Church in Saint-Jacques-de-la-Lande and for his friendship.
And finally, all those who are currently involved in our workshop, for their commitment and patience, as well as the teams who have come before them, ever since the office was first created.

# IMPRINT

Cover: Antoine Guilhem-Ducléon, Wall in the Landscape

Design and Setting: Jean-Pierre Pranlas-Descours and Zhaoying Zhu with Maxime Léger
and Flore Teyssendier de la Serve
Translation: Jean-Pierre Pranlas-Descours
Proofreading: Irene Murphy Lewis, Julie Heathcote-Smith
Copy Editor: Lee Holt
Lithography: Bild1Druck Berlin
Printed in the European Union.

Bibliographic information published by the Deutsche Nationalbibliothek.
The Deutsche Nationalbibliothek lists this publication in the Deutsche Nationalbibliografie. Detailed
bibliographic data are available on the Internet at http://dnb.d-nb.de.

jovis Verlag GmbH
Lützowstraße 33
10785 Berlin

www.jovis.de

jovis books are available worldwide in select bookstores. Please contact your nearest bookseller or visit www.
jovis.de for information concerning your local distribution.

ISBN 978-3-86859-720-2